2/10/3

Help me spread the word!

Nathan Stz.

Strategic Clarity

The Essentials of High-level Selling

by Nathan E. Steele

Strategic Clarity Press, Inc.

Copyright 2002 by Strategic Clarity, Inc. All rights reserved.
Published by Strategic Clarity Press, Inc.
ISBN 0-9720376-0-8

No part of this publication may be reproduced, stored in a retrieval system or transmitted in any form or by any means, electronic, mechanical, photocopying, recording, scanning or otherwise, except as permitted under Sections 107 or 108 of the 1976 United States Copyright Act, without either the prior written permission of the Publisher, or authorization through payment of the appropriate per-copy fee to the Copyright Clearance Center, 222 Rosewood Drive, Danvers, MA 01923, (978) 750-8400, fax (978) 750-4744. Requests to the Publisher for permission should be addressed to the Permissions Department, Strategic Clarity Press, c/o Promise Publishing Co., P. O. Box 10759, Santa Ana, CA 92711, 970 927-0255, fax 970 927-0256, email permissions@strategicclarity.com.

This publication is designed to provide accurate and authoritative information in regard to the subject matter covered. It is sold with the understanding that the publisher is not engaged in rendering professional services. If professional advice or other expert assistance is required, the services of a competent professional person should be sought.

Printed in the United States of America on acid free paper.

10 9 8 7 6 5 4 3 2

The author makes no case for why and how this book should be interpreted for greatest profit. It is introduced as a platform for the consideration of those involved in the endeavor, and the interpretation is up to the reader.

The case is presented. When all is said and done, Strategic Clarity is no more or less than the search for broader and more creative avenues of thinking.

In sales, we frequently fall short of the line we draw for ourselves. Nonetheless, we must continue to draw that line in such a way that our continuing growth is assured. Then, in hindsight, we will look back and realize that we have gone much farther than we could ever have imagined.

Table of Contents

Preface — i
Strategic Clarity — v

Introduction
Introduction — ix
Traditional Selling is Dead — xi
The Selling Environment — xxi
The Future of Selling — xxv

Create Demand
Customer Value Orientation — 1
Feature, Benefit, Value — 8
Understanding Value — 16
Risk and Value Profile — 19
Key Business Drivers — 29
The Value Chain — 31
The Buying Process — 35
Value Based Pricing — 41
Summary — 51

Pursue Opporunity
Introduction to Strategic Planning — 55
Strategy Defined — 60
Building a Strategy Statement — 66
Types of Strategies — 71
Selecting the Right Strategy — 82
The Corporate Agenda — 95
Sales Planning Formats — 101
Defensive Countermeasures — 108
Profiling and Situation Analysis — 120
Summary — 142

Pursue Opporunity — 53

Relationship Management 143
    Relationship Management 145
    The Personal Agenda 151
    The Professional Agenda 155
    Creating Momentum 160
    Power and Politics 167
    Detection First 174
    Power Brokers and the Inner Circle 180
    Identifying the Political Structure 184
    Political Activity 187
    Building a Political Plan 190
    Summary 191

Epilogue 193
    Executive Evangelism 195
    Scripting the Call 209
    Competency Development 226
    Recommended Reading 229

Preface

This book is the compilation of what I have learned over the last ten years of training high-level sales teams. Over the years, I have been exposed to literally thousands of good ideas that help salespeople win more business. I have put in this one book the best of those lessons.

There is no single book that covers all of the essential things every high-level salesperson must be able to do. Those three things are Create Demand, Pursue Opportunity and Relationship Management. These three things provide salespeople with the ability to apply their business acumen, act competitively and develop those relationships that bring with them competitive advantage.

The thinking in this book is not new or unique. It is not structured on some mnemonic acronym allowing easy recall. It is not tactically focused to assure that the salesperson says the right thing at the right time to their customers.

The thinking in this book is meant to enhance the aspiring high-level salesperson's ability to think critically and make good decisions. It is designed to illuminate business-level thinking to the point where the application is de rigueur; it becomes the natural way of proceeding. It is the common sense thinking that every high-level salesperson should be able to do without referring back to some acronym-led sales process.

This book is not a process; it is a way of thinking. *Process* attempts to breakdown the sales situation into sequential steps, one following the other. *Process* attempts to provide sales managers with greater insight into what is happening in their selling environment. Replacing process for the salesperson's ability to think and perform is a dangerous philosophy.

The readers who pick up this book will be able make better decisions without referring to a process. They will be able to make better sense out of the complexity that is the sales environment. Just as a lawyer is able to parse a complex legal question into its relevant pieces, this methodology provides readers with the ability to understand their sales situation.

I must thank all those who have taught me, who have provided me the time and encouragement to compile, in an orderly manner, this book. There are the thousands of salespeople who have shared their struggles and ideas with me who deserve my thanks. There are my friends whose patience and interest sustained me in the construction of this book. There is my wife, Heidi, and my family, who deserve a great deal of credit for the existence of this book.

I must also take responsibility for any errors. With the help of so many friends and colleagues, whose advice and guidance are so valued, any omission, confusion or errors that remain are completely my fault. They are likely the result of my personal limitation to listen, a critical talent for any salesperson.

As I began this book, my goal was to include every facet of high-level sales success that I considered central and important. As I began writing, I quickly realized that to achieve that goal would require a tome of 800 or 900 pages.

The original thinking was comprehensive but the final product is the essentials.

Your feedback is welcome. As much as anyone, I recognize the value of other's ideas and criticism. You are welcome to add your voice to this work by emailing me directly at www.strategicclarity.com.

Strategic Clarity

It is possible to reach Strategic Clarity in any sales situation. Strategic Clarity is the point where your understanding of the sales situation gives you the insight necessary to win business. By capturing enough relevant information, it is possible to fully understand where you are in the sales situation and recognize what you need to do to win the business.

This is the point of consilience, the point where everything comes together. This is the point of Strategic Clarity. To most people, winning and losing in sales is a mystery. Even when they win, they have only a vague idea of why they won. By reaching this point of consilience, you achieve a point of clarity that defines your path to winning business.

"If you cannot articulate, you cannot understand. If you cannot understand, you cannot control." This guiding principle means that if you cannot describe the sales situation, you cannot begin to control it. This means that the first step to achieving Strategic Clarity is the collection and analysis of information, articulating the selling environment. With the articulation comes understanding and with understanding comes the ability to control. When you are in position to control a sales situation, you are in position to win.

Winning is more than taking an order. Winning means that the customer sees great value in the relationship with you. Winning means that you were able to eliminate price as a buying issue. Winning means that you are in position for more business from the same customer. Winning means that your competitor was completely unaware of their loss, until it was too late.

Nothing is quite as satisfying as winning for all the right reasons. You won because you provided the customer with the motivation to purchase. You won because the customer used your logic, your words to justify their purchase.

Is it possible to reach this state of consilience in every sales campaign? In selling, consilience is the point of convergence of three key factors giving a salesperson greater control of the sales situation. They were able to establish a compelling, business related value proposition. They out-gunned their competition with a masterful strategy, brilliantly executed. They positioned themselves and their offering with the most powerful people in the account. These three things give a salesperson the ability to leverage a different kind of competitive advantage, sales excellence.

These key factors are Creating Value, Pursue Opportunity and Relationship Management. Each of these involves the salesperson's ability to articulate, understand and control the sales situation, and do so in a way that their competition has no hope of winning.

Consilience is possible in every sales situation. It might not seem possible to salespeople saddled with traditional sales cultures and outdated thinking. It might not seem possible to the salesperson who sells by the "quote and hope" method. It might not seem possible to those whose customer universe is too vast or internal reporting requirements too large. However, consilience is possible in every sales situation. Once you learn the language of Strategic Clarity, consilience becomes your goal in every sales campaign.

Consilience can be expensive, but the rewards are enormous. One of the rewards would be a sales organization operating at peak levels. Another would be closing rates approaching 100%. Another would be generous profit margins, happy customers and more salespeople reaching quota more often.

Strategic Clarity's mission is to provide men and women the means by which they can achieve greater control of their sales campaigns, their business and their lives. We will never achieve this mission just as no sales organization will ever close 100% of their opportunities. However, improvements grow exponentially over time and rewards multiply.

Introduction

There are no easy answers worth knowing. There are no shortcuts to success. Successful salespeople are successful because of the consistent application of their growing competencies and the highest standards of ethics and professionalism. They are successful because of hard work.

The ideas and methodology in this book come from the many years I have spent working with major corporations throughout the world. I have worked with scores of companies including Ericsson, EDS, Sprint, Sun Microsystems, Intel, Cisco, Microsoft, Qwest and Accenture. In addition to the large companies, I have worked with many small companies. I have worked in industries as diverse as Software, IT Services, Computer Hardware, Telecom, Healthcare and Auto Parts. I have worked with companies that dominate their space as well as companies doing battle with Goliath. It has been my privilege to meet and work with thousands of sales people throughout North America, South America, Asia and Europe, in more than 30 countries.

I wrote this book to fill a void. There is no single book that I am aware of (and I've been looking for years) that lays out *all* of the competencies required to succeed at the highest levels of selling. There are great books and training programs that help salespeople with tactical selling skills. There are books about value, business language, calling high, politics and strategic selling.

However, no single book covers all of the competencies necessary for high-level sales success.

All of the selling competencies that are necessary for success are in this book. They fall into three broad categories. To be a successful high-level salesperson, you must be able to do these three things with a high level of competence. They are *Create Demand*, *Pursue Opportunity* and *Relationship Management*.

This book is not about tactical selling skills. Skills like overcoming objections, advancing the customer dialog, presentation skills, asking for the order, negotiation and closing techniques need to be present in the reader who picks up this book. The ability to do all of these tactical skills to some level of competence is a requirement for a high-level salesperson.

Even though most of what you know about selling is a requirement for success at high-level selling, the inappropriate application of traditional sales skills is no longer acceptable. Some salespeople are too overbearing, too gregarious for decent company. Their enthusiasm or personalities seem to fly in the face of socially acceptable behavior

Customers, particularly large customers, are tired of anti-social, sales-types and seldom tolerate this type of behavior for long, particularly at the executive level. This type of salesperson is either outdated or best left to those who have to do business with them.

Customers are intelligent and interested not solely in buying, but in solving some problem or being able to improve their company's performance. They do not want to be sold.

Traditional Selling is Dead

Traditional selling is dead. The traditional role the selling organization has played for the last hundred years has been struggling to keep up with changing customer expectations, changing technology and ever commoditizing markets. *The economic forces that have been evident for the last 5 years will in the next 5 years forever change the form and the function of the professional salesperson and their selling organization.*

Traditional selling has been, at its most basic level, a function of information dissemination. Companies launch salespeople as their primary conduit of information. Companies train salespeople in products and technology and in traditional sales approaches. Salespeople use a myriad of sales techniques to advance dialog from the interest level to the buying level. Their intention has been *commercial* in nature, to find new customers, or to win new business from existing customers.

The problem is that the essential role of a selling organization, information dissemination, is fast becoming an unprofitable function. The investment companies make in the selling organization have been negatively affected by falling prices and shrinking margins. This leaves little money to pay for the higher level selling efforts those companies want and need. To offset the price squeeze and profit shrinkage, companies ask their salespeople to accomplish more with fewer resources. Taken from the perspective of a CFO, it would be appropriate to suggest that if a selling organization is incapable of selling profitably, then there is little use left for the selling organization or the salesperson.

There is little room in any company for non-economic functions. Every function inside a company's business process map must add some measurable value to the product. As raw materials advance through a company, each stop along the way to final product must add some measurable value. If not, they will eliminate or replace the function.

Using sophisticated financial tools, companies are eliminating non-performing investments. The purpose of Business Process Reengineering over the last 10 years has been to eliminate non-performing business processes and increase the efficiencies of a company's value chain. The traditional selling organization, the information dissemination organization, is a non-performing asset, in danger of extinction.

Accelerating Change

Markets change. This, of course, should come as no surprise. The rate of change is accelerating. This, as well, should come as no surprise. However, few people have thought through the concept of accelerating change and internalized the implications for businesses and consumers. Fewer still have thought through the challenge of accelerating change and the impact on the selling organization and its salespeople.

Change is evident in virtually every market, in every corner of the world. In spite of the intellectual acknowledgement that markets have changed and that change is accelerating, many companies continue to cling to traditional selling and their traditional selling organizations.

Over the years, we have seen customer expectations change. The choices that customers face today are exponentially greater than they were 5 or 10 years ago.

Competition among companies and between industries has been changing as well. Companies now compete head-to-head with companies that used to be in different industries altogether.

For example, in 1990, EDS, Cap-Gemini and CSC were virtually the only choices for large corporations to consider if they were thinking of outsourcing their information technology infrastructure. Today, the choices have grown to include Accenture and most of the other major consulting firms, and Telecom companies such as Sprint and Qwest (naming only a few). In addition, there are hosts of small companies getting into IT outsourcing as Application Software Providers. These companies will lease the software applications, design the infrastructure and provide the computer equipment and the communication network. With little capital of their own, these small shops are effectively competing in the same markets as EDS, Cap-Gemini and CSC.

Technology has changed. What used to be large, bulky and slow, is now fast and fits nicely in a pocket. The computing power that used to describe a supercomputer now costs less than $800. By 2000, microprocessor chip speed surpassed one Gigahertz. Scientists are now working on photon-based microprocessors, as opposed to electron-based. They are expecting to exceed microprocessor speeds spoken in terms of *terahertz* by 2010-12. These technology changes have made their way into every industry in every organized economy in the world.

Not only has technology seen exponential growth but, in addition, the cost of that technology has dropped as well. Several technologies, particularly in computing and telecommunications, have seen *economically disruptive* breakthroughs. For example, Level 3, a telecommunications provider, saw the changes coming and began building a backbone, city-to-city telecommunication network infrastructure, using new telecommunication technology. In a relatively short time, they were able to build a network that brought together Asia, Pacific Rim, North America, South America and Europe. Even though you may have never heard of them, Level 3's network capacity is large enough to carry all of the world's voice and data communications. They have accomplished this at an investment cost of less than one-one/hundredth of older technologies.

These accelerating changes will affect all industries, not just high tech industries. No company will be able to be anything but early adopters of new technologies. New technology and the dropping cost of new technology will rapidly translate into strategic advantage.

The Threat to Traditional Selling

Three forces will change forever the form and the function of every sales organization and every sales professional in every company in every major economy on this planet.

First, we will see the full integration of the internet into existing business process models by established companies. Next, the increasing power of technologies will force companies to reevaluate the role of selling in their organization. Third, the increasing commoditization of markets will force companies to either accept commodity status or find other more effective ways of differentiating themselves. These three factors are combining to eliminate the need for traditional selling skills, traditional salespeople and traditional selling organizations.

Internet as a Business Model

The integration of the internet as a business model into traditional companies will increasingly replace business processes that require input from the selling organization. Internet based businesses such as Amazon, eBay and Yahoo created unique, customer oriented tools, giving customers the ability to take care of themselves 24/7, a level of convenience never before seen. The tools they created also gave their customers a feeling of greater intimacy without the high cost of a selling organization.

The integration of the internet into traditional business processes will create never before imagined tools and conveniences for customers. Integration of the internet as a business tool will allow companies to develop business processes that will help them create close relationships with many more customers. It will allow companies to broaden their markets and find new customers for a fraction of the cost of a selling organization. It will allow companies to deliver their products and services in fully customized ways. It will allow companies to run their businesses efficiently, creating new forms of savings and profitability. Companies will be able to forecast with pinpoint accuracy current levels of demand. Companies will be able to shorten the distance between raw material and customer, and do so with a one-to-one feeling of customized personalization for all of their customers.

Most companies have not begun to examine their existing business processes in the context of the internet. We see intranets and software tools that use the internet as the communication network. We see the corporate presence website and order-entry portals. We even see public and private exchange sites where companies can buy, sell and handle their accounting for a host of different products and services. What we have not seen yet, is a serious examination of current business processes and the invention of new business processes fully capitalizing on the internet.

Technology

In combination with the adoption of the internet into existing business models, software, hardware and communication networks will become more useful, powerful and faster. There will be a surge in productivity gains from the use of newer technologies. Much of the productivity gains will come on the demand side of a company's value chain. This is the point of contact of the traditional selling organization. Portions of a traditional salesperson's duties face elimination as more customers become accustomed to a technological interface with their suppliers. The increasing speed of the microprocessor, the dropping cost of servers, the increasing power and usefulness of software, the speed and ubiquity of the connection to the internet will combine to create useful tools for customers to manage their own relationships with their suppliers.

Increasing Commoditization

The fact that products do not provide companies and salespeople with the type of differentiation that they once did has brought whole industry segments and markets into a state of commoditization. Companies have traditionally fought this trend by investing in Research and Development. The difficulty is that the normal advantage enjoyed through technological innovation is more fleeting now than ever. Where companies could create a year, maybe two, of product superiority, the time advantage has shrunk to months, if at all.

Another traditional way that companies have countered commoditization is with the integration of commoditized products into solution sets. By combining a commoditized product or technology into a package or solution set, focused on solving a customer problem, a new period of differentiation is established. Using these solution sets, companies could once more exploit a period of differentiation. Today, of course, every competitor, almost as an economic fact-of-life, will respond in kind, limiting the potential gain.

These three forces, the integration of the internet into new and existing business processes, the advancement of technology and the further commoditization of products, will bring a challenge to the selling organization never seen before. Nothing in the last 40 years will equal the challenge sales will face in the next 5 years. *Traditional selling is dead.*

Selling in the Next Economy

These forces will *forever change the form and the function of every sales organization and every sales professional in every company in every major economy on this planet.* What is changing, and will continue to change, will cause whole companies to reexamine what role salespeople can, or should, play in their company. The inevitable changes will cause whole companies to consider doing away with the function that we have known traditionally as sales. It will force salespeople to change the way they do business.

Market changes in many industries have already forced companies to cut back on their investment in traditional sales approaches. Those cutbacks have forced selling organizations to expand territories and reduce the number of people working with major accounts, but the form and function of sales has stubbornly remained unchanged.

The future of selling is in its economic justification. As with any other investment, a company's investment in sales has to provide an economic yield. The salesperson must be individually responsible for not just selling, per se, but selling profitably. In order for the salesperson to sell profitably on a continuing basis, they must be able to create a measurable financial return for their customer that is greater than their product's value. By creating measurable customer value, they create a measurable value for their company. By creating value for their company, they provide an economic justification for their company's investment in selling. Without a measurable financial return, the sales organization is vulnerable.

Selling and the selling organization have enjoyed a measure of insulation from the sweeping changes that corporations have endured over the last decade. Now, the changes will focus almost entirely on the customer end of the value chain, the province of the sales department.

You may believe that these changes will never happen for any number of reasons; or that they will never happen in your industry or your company. You may wish to think that the world does not really change that much or that fast. But, it has, it does and it will continue to do so.

The question is not "if?" but "when?" and "how much?" Given these predictions, the relevant question is, what potential solutions are there to compete more effectively, as professional salespeople and as professional selling organizations, in the next economy?

The Selling Environment

The foundation of selling has a *Commercial Intent*, the intention of engaging customers in the consideration of doing business. The concept of solicitation and persuasion is the role and the art of selling. To solicit is to ask or seek earnestly. To be solicitous, however, is to be anxious or concerned; full of desire and eagerness. Salespeople try to induce, attract, tempt, entice, allure charm, cajole and tantalize. A salesperson's job is to influence, prompt, incite, pressure, provoke, encourage, advocate, exhort and lobby their prospects and customers to do business.

Inside the selling environment, salespeople pursue economic fulfillment for themselves and their companies. They are trained or untrained. They are supported or unsupported. What is clear is that they will face many challenges. Some of them will rise to the challenge, and others may fall away.

Not to be *fully armed and fully prepared* for the selling environment leaves the salesperson *disabled*. To enter the selling environment disabled, in a state of partial preparation, is nearly the same as not being prepared at all. Success will come at a greater cost than had they been fully prepared.

So, what does fully prepared mean? It means that a *whole company* is operating in concert with a well-trained sales organization. It means that both are ready for engagement in the selling environment. It means that the sales force is not only *tactically adept*, but *strategically capable*, as well.

If you were determined to climb Mt. Everest, what kind of preparation would you go through to assure your success? In the absence of that preparation, what would be your chance of success? What would be the cost of failure? If your life depended on your planning and preparation, what corners would you cut?

Of course, you would not cut any corners at all. You would study the mountain and previous expeditions, the weather, and the maps. You would consult with people who have successfully made it to the top. You would, based upon the information available to you, select the approach up the mountain that would most likely succeed. Based on the approach you chose, you would prepare yourself physically and mentally for the arduous climb. You would equip yourself, not only for the most likely scenarios of weather, but for contingencies that others found to be relevant. You would never mount an assault on Mt. Everest without full preparation.

In selling, in those opportunities crucial to your success, you should never go off to compete without a similar level of preparedness. You may not feel that you have adequate time to plan or adequate support from your company. If that is the case, then perhaps you should not pursue the opportunity at all. Most salespeople would still pursue the opportunity, and some may even succeed, but the likelihood of success would be very small.

Few companies would arrive at the real reason for the failure. They might blame price discounting by their competitor to cannibalistic levels. They might blame politics or existing relationships for their failure. They may even blame the salesperson. However, the real reason for failure is most often lack of preparation and bad decision-making based on faulty information.

In October 2001, Lockheed Martin won the largest contract ever awarded by the United States government for the next generation of fighter aircraft. The initial value of the contract was $200 billion dollars, an amount that would exceed the GDP of most of the world's economies. The eventual value over the life of the product could reach over $1,000 billion, or $1 trillion.

In the competition, Lockheed Martin was competing with Boeing, a formidable competitor. Some financial analysts had suggested that if Lockheed Martin had not won, they would have gone out of business. The competition involved thousands of people, and millions of dollars over several years. Even if their corporate existence had not relied on the winning of the contract, this was a big deal.

If you were the salesperson for Lockheed Martin, how much research and analysis, would you do to build the plan to win the business? What corners would you cut in your planning effort?

If you were responsible for winning the business, you would do everything necessary to insure that you won. You would not cut any corners at all. As if your life depended on your research and analysis, your plan and the execution of your plan, you would never cut any corners.

<u>Strategic Clarity: The Essentials of Professional Selling</u> will help you win those opportunities that are vital to your success. This book is the thinking, format and the methodology *minimally required* to compete at the highest

levels of selling, those mission-critical, live-or-die opportunities.

The Future of Selling

Traditional selling relies on three traditional competitive advantages. *Product Excellence* is the differentiator designed and built into the products or the services. *Economic Excellence* is the ability for a company to offer, through their own rigorous internal processes, a competitive price for a quality product. *Industry Presence Excellence* is the development of a quality image for the company in the market place.

These traditional competitive advantages are the responsibility of companies' marketing organizations that seek to create products for exploitable market niches or to build an image in their chosen markets. These competitive advantages also involve a company's manufacturing and operational team with their ability to produce a quality product at a more competitive price level.

For the sales organization, it is a luxury to have these advantages all coordinated into one compelling offering. When the product is superior, the price is cheaper and the company's image and reputation are impressive, salespeople feel as if they cannot lose. They can beat their competitors with an unmatched product and price and they have a positive image with the customer. How can they lose?

The reality for salespeople, even when all of these advantages are coordinated into one unbeatable offering, is that they can still lose the business. Even though their product is clearly better, their price is lower and they are unencumbered by an unknown brand name, they can still lose.

The final source of competitive advantage is nontraditional and less accepted than the first three competitive advantages. The final source of competitive advantage is *Sales Excellence*, the salespeople themselves. What salespeople bring to the competition can determine whether they win the business or lose the business.

Sales Excellence

Sales Excellence is defined as the salesperson's ability to better control the sales situation. A higher level of control brings with it the ability to win business on the terms most favorable to their company and the customer. A higher level of control brings with it the ability to eliminate or manipulate the competition. A higher level of control in the selling situation is the combination of two primary areas of concern to the salesperson: *Customer Issues* and the *Competitive Issues*.

Customer Issues

Customer issues begin with the product or the service the customer feels best satisfies their needs. Here the salesperson is concerned with the features of the offering and the customer's specifications of what they intend to buy. A salesperson's ability to gain some measure of control in helping the customer define these buying criteria is important to their ability to win business.

The next area a salesperson seeks to control, in relationship to customer issues, is the business impact of their offering. There is an implied business improvement when a customer buys; that improvement may be in the form of productivity or improved business processes. Sometimes the implied improvement applies directly to the customer's own internal business operations and might sometimes apply to their ability to compete better in their markets. If the contemplated purchase is large and central to a customer's business plan, then the customer's focus is on their ability to compete in their markets and the competitive salesperson needs to recognize this and position themselves accordingly. The salesperson that helps the customer define, and measure the impact of the purchase would be in a better position than the salesperson that is unaware of the business impact to the customer.

The final area of customer issues that a salesperson needs to be concerned with is the political environment within the customer organization. The salesperson's ability to recognize the informal, invisible structure of politics in the customer organization could potentially better position themselves than their unaware competitor. They would be able to act in accordance with the customer's cultural values and seek the support of the most powerful people in the organization. The salesperson that is able to garner the support of the politically powerful people would have a commanding position compared to their competition.

The salesperson who is able to gain some degree of control over the customer issues, the buying criteria, the definition of the business impact, and the political environment, is a salesperson who has gained a higher level of control of the sales situation, a higher level of Sales Excellence. They are playing a more effective offense and are out-positioning their competition. A good offense is a good defense in selling. However, it is only half the game. The professional salesperson must also play defense.

Competitive Issues

The competitive issues in a sales situation begin with the competition's offering, their stuff versus your stuff. The high-level salesperson needs to be cognizant of the specifics and the character of the competition's offering. The salesperson, in order to gain a higher level of control in the sales situation, needs to know the strengths and the weakness of the competitor's offering. They will need to be able to capitalize professionally on the competitor's weaknesses, while discrediting their strengths.

The next level of concern with regard to the competitive aspects of a selling situation is the need for the salesperson to play a proactive form of in-your-face defense. What are the predictable tactics of the competitor and what can they do proactively to negate these anticipated tactics? What kind of strategy does the competition typically employ and how can it be defeated? Sales organizations are predictable, having a tendency to replicate those activities that have brought them success in the past. Familiarizing themselves with those tendencies can give the professional salesperson a commanding edge in the competition.

Finally, in order to achieve a higher level of control in the sales situation, the high-level salesperson needs to develop an effective strategy, or approach. The strategy is the primary approach that the salesperson will use in the execution of their sales campaign. The strategy is developed based on the analysis of the selling environment, including the customer and their issues and the competitive aspects of the selling situation. Whether you are weak or strong, competing with one competitor or a host of

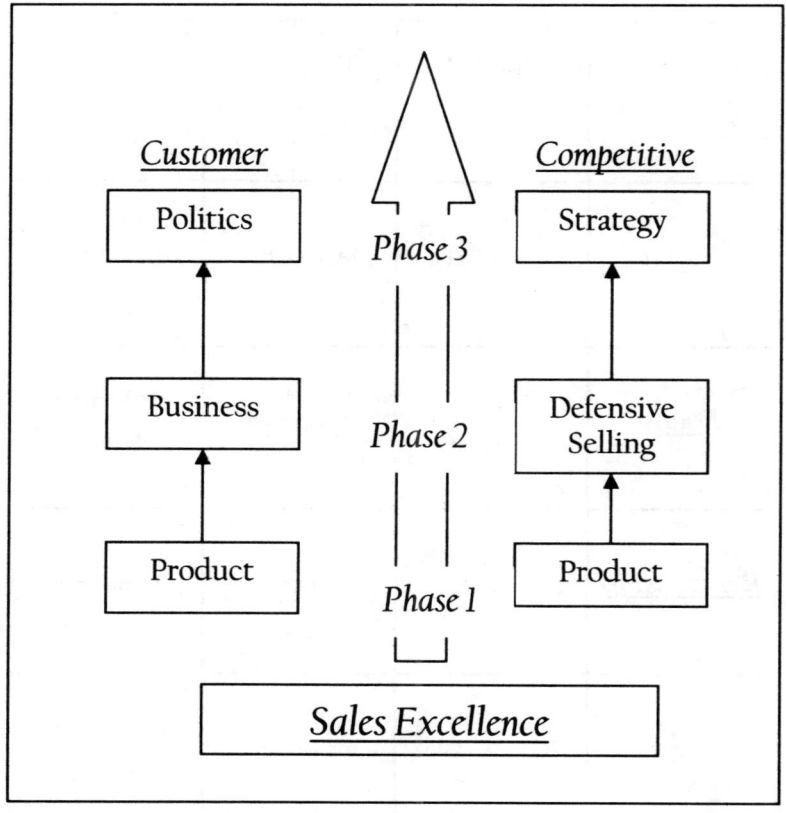

competitors, your strategy is critical to your success. It gives strength to your sales campaign and, done well, optimizes your resources.

By combining these components, both offensive and defensive, into a comprehensive sales plan, the result is a powerful sales campaign designed to gain greater control of the sales situation.

Sales Proficiency Matrix

	Phase I	Phase II	Phase III
Intent	Consideration	Make a Sale	Repeat Business
Focus	Product Offering	Customer	Customer's Business
Relationship	Casual	Personal	Connected
Value	Human Catalog	Problem Solver	Competitive Advantage

Phase I

The Phase I salesperson is concerned with getting in the door and getting their offerings in front of the customer. Their preferred method of finding these customers or prospects is through a lead generation marketing program that pre-qualifies some interest in a prospect. They will use the door most open to them. They will do whatever is required to get to the proposal step. They will submit their proposal and then hope the customer calls them back with a purchase order. The Phase I salesperson lives in a state of "Quote and Hope".

All sales motion ceases once the proposal is under consideration by the prospect. The focus is on the offering and the features of the offering. Their relationship with the customer is casual and *likable* in nature. They must be likable since they believe that people do business with people they like. The value they represent to their customers lies in their familiarity with their offerings.

Phase II

In Phase II, the intention is to close business as quickly as possible and move on to the next prospect. They are tactically proficient in closing techniques, and accomplished in the other sales tactics that they have learned over the years. They do not take "no" for an answer, they overcome objections. They are able to give the standard presentation and know how to advance the sales campaign in the face of tepid interest. Their focus is on the customer and the customer's experience dealing with them. They are prone to do anything within reason to create goodwill with virtually anyone in the customer organization. The value they represent to the customer is that they are capable of providing not just a product offering, but also an entire, end-to-end solution.

Phase III

The Phase III salesperson is able to use a consultative approach in their sales campaign. They approach, not with their product in mind or the thought of closing an order, but with the idea that there might be an opportunity for a long-term mutually profitable relationship with the customer. They are able to execute a highly competitive sales campaign, building effective strategies and proactively using defensive countermeasures to defeat their competition. Their intention is to develop a partnership with the whole customer organization. Their focus is on the customer's marketplace, developing a much more intimate understanding of the customer's customer and the customer's competition. The relationships they build are mutually beneficial and take into account personal and professional agendas. They understand the political atmosphere of the customer organization and are capable of professionally operating in that environment. Their value is based on their ability to deliver a measurable financial result to the customer.

The Challenge to Selling

Phase I selling is a profitable enterprise when properly managed and compensated. Phase III selling is also a very profitable enterprise when properly supported and executed. However, in most companies, Phase II selling dominates, and unfortunately, Phase II selling is either *unprofitable* or will become so in the next few years.

The reason that Phase II is unprofitable is that these salespeople rely heavily on traditional competitive advantages. They use product excellence as their preferred differentiator. In the absence of a differentiated product, they rely on the name of their company. When that does not work, they fall back on price discounting, sacrificing margins for revenue. If they are unable to differentiate *how* they sell it (*sales excellence*), they *must* differentiate it by *how much* they sell it for. Price becomes the differentiator.

Ironically, most companies want salespeople to sell as much as they possibly can. In most companies, a salesperson doing $40 million in revenue at 1% margins is compensated more than a salesperson who sells $10 million at 40% margins. The salesperson operating with 1% margins is sent off to *President's Club* somewhere in Hawaii for a week of fun, while the other one stays home and pays the bill. If you were the CFO of this company, who would you rather have working for you?

Companies tend to replicate the sales practices that have brought them success. What brought them success in years past, is what they believe will bring them success today. As a result, successful salespeople become sales managers who define the role of the salesperson. They hire, train, and coach salespeople to do what they did to achieve their success. Many of those managers, however, met with success under different market conditions and were able to profitably employ traditional, Phase II selling skills. Considering the increasing competitiveness of the market and the technological advances of the last few years, it is no longer economically feasible to use the Phase II approach.

The Solution

It is imperative that companies get out of Phase II selling as quickly as possible. Move as much of that selling activity up into Phase III before your competition does. Move the remaining Phase II selling activity down to the commoditized marketplace of Phase I. Companies should engage in Phase II sales activity *only when necessary.*

Phase I represents a capitulation to commoditized, price sensitive competition. Standardize as much of the selling process as possible. Compensate the sales force to handle as many customers as possible, as consistently as possible. Allocate as much of the customer interface to Internet-based software tools. Allow the customer to manage as much of their relationship with you as possible.

Phase III Selling

The Phase III sales professional needs to be able to do three things at a world-class level.

First, *Create Demand*, the sales approach is focused not on the offering itself, but rather on the creation of measurable value using the measurements of the customer. In the absence of the creation of customer value, the sales function becomes less profitable and ultimately ends up in the commoditized Phase I approach.

Next, the Phase III salesperson needs to be able to *Pursue Opportunity* with a high degree of competitiveness. When a competitive sales situation presents itself, the salesperson needs to be able to build effective strategies to defeat their competition. They need to be able to execute the defensive countermeasures that disable their competitor. They need to be able to recognize, when they should compete, and when they should not.

Finally, the Phase III salesperson needs to be able to be a *Relationship Manager,* building and maintaining professional relationships, with the *right people*. They need to be able to understand people better and more quickly than their competitors. They need to be able to engage the customer's personal and professional agendas in their sales campaigns. They need to know how to build momentum. They need to be able to recognize, who is and who is not, powerful in the sales situation and do so with accuracy and speed. They need to be able to capitalize on their relationship building activities by establishing relationships with the right people, the powerful people.

Create Demand. Pursue Opportunity, Relationship Management. These three things create *Sales Excellence.* The salesperson must be able to do these three things at a very high level of excellence, or they and their company will lose to the commoditized marketplace of Phase I.

Create Demand

Create Demand is the consultative approach high-level salespeople need to change the character of their relationship with customers from a product perspective to a Customer Value Orientation. It requires that they understand the financial impact of their offering. To do this, they must be able to identify the customer's risk profile and Key Business Drivers. They must understand the customer's Value Chain. They must also be aware of where the customer is in their Buying Process.

Customer Value Orientation

Somewhere in this world, a sales team has earned the right to go to the top. They have obtained a meeting with the CEO or the senior-most executives in the prospect organization. The meeting represents a huge opportunity, one that the sales team has worked for months to schedule. The moment has finally arrived.

The sales team's preparation is impeccable. The presentation will bring out the important features of the proposed platform. The slides for the presentation are all in order. There are slides to establish credibility; slides to show they care. Overall, they have prepared a very professional and well-thought-out presentation. They feel confident going into the meeting.

The moment has come. The audience arrives. The usual light comments and introductions are cordial and brief. The sales team's chief supporter is personally invested in the project. He opens the meeting and turns the audience over to the presenter and the presentation begins....

Within minutes, it becomes clear that all the research and effort is missing the mark. The CEO is trying to be polite, but the presenter exceeded his attention span for irrelevancy within seconds. Maybe it was the overhead photograph of the headquarters building. Maybe it was the animated picture of the product dancing the Macarena.

Maybe it was the third slide on specifications. What the sales team thought would be a riveting, engaging, even entertaining presentation quickly degraded into a miserable, uncomfortable presentation.

No one wants to be there. Large moments of silence follow the presenter's feeble attempts as he tries to engage the audience. Their sponsor shrinks to half his former size. If decorum allowed, he would be hiding under his chair. Moreover, the presenter still has 42 slides to go. Finally, well before the last slide hits the screen, the CEO says as politely as possible, "I think we've seen enough."

What happened? Where did they go wrong? If you have not been in this type of situation before, consider yourself lucky. If you have, you probably know where you went wrong.

As salespeople, you are trained in product, in technology, in what differentiates you from the competition, in your stuff. As human beings, we all have the natural tendency to want to talk about ourselves. In our example, the sales team assumed that they had permission to talk about their favorite subjects, their stuff and themselves. Maybe that was exactly what the audience expected of them. They came, they talked, they met expectations, and they bored the audience to exhaustion and, mercifully, the presentation was cut short. They may even win the business. However, what did they gain? What privilege did they earn? What currency did they gain through the experience? What could they possibly have done better?

A.C. Nielsen had been a devoted IBM customer for many years. The world knows them as the TV ratings people, but their major business is market research, information and analysis for the consumer products and services industries. Through their exhaustive research using both information technologies and point-of-sale canvassing, they provide important information to companies. They are now a division of VNU N.V., a $3 billion revenue company based in Europe, but at the time A.C. Nielsen was an independent, publicly traded company suffering from declining revenues and margins; increasing competition that had been eroding their market share.

In an effort to improve their ability to perform, the senior executives of A.C. Nielsen were considering a decision to outsource their entire information technology (IT) infrastructure. IBM had been a part of the A.C. Nielsen family for many years, having sold them virtually their entire infrastructure. There were long standing relationships between the IBM people and their counterparts in A.C. Nielsen. Even though IBM would have to buy back A.C. Nielsen's IT infrastructure, IBM would be able to amortize the system over many years and continue to reap the rewards of future expenditures.

The final two companies in the competition were IBM and EDS (Electronic Data Systems) based in Plano, Texas. EDS was very comfortable in the IT outsourcing business, having invented the industry many years before. Most computer companies, during that era, thought only of building and selling their equipment, along with software, integration and services. EDS leveraged their computer expertise to build and operate a customer's entire IT infrastructure. In effect, EDS sells the output of IT, rather than the infrastructure.

The final showdown was set for the end of the buying process where the executives of A.C. Nielsen would watch the presentations of the two finalists on the same day; two hours for IBM followed by two hours for EDS. IBM presented first. For two hours, the executives patiently listened, watched and considered their options.

During the break between the two presentations, the feedback to EDS was that IBM's presentation had essentially met expectations. However, it was too technical for most of the executives to follow, but it had confirmed what A.C. Nielsen seemed to believe; that IBM could do the work.

Realizing that their presentation would delve deeply into the technology, infrastructure and the scope of service, EDS knew they had a problem. The problem was that their presentation would mirror the one that the executives had already seen. Their presentation would not differentiate them, would not set them apart. Their presentation would not enable them to win the business.

EDS faced a very hard decision. Should they go out and do the presentation as planned, or should they change the presentation to something entirely different? If they decided to change the presentation to something different, what would their message be? If they changed the presentation, they would have no message, no slides and no collateral to support whatever that message would be. Complicating things, the EDS team was not the incumbent and the advantage in these types of situations usually goes to the incumbent.

EDS had already invested over $1,000,000 in cost-of-sales for this campaign alone. Winning this deal would mean revenues of hundreds of millions of dollars over the life of the contract. The careers of many people were at-risk on this one deal.

Put yourself in EDS' position. What would you do if you were the salesperson? Would you proceed as planned, or would you change your presentation and assume an unknown risk? Would you play it safe or change your presentation? If you decided to change your presentation, what would you say?

You might begin by listing the things you cannot talk about. You cannot talk about yourself. You cannot talk about your offering. You cannot talk about your company. Talking about those things would not set you apart from IBM. You cannot talk about your credibility or experience. You are already considered credible, because you are there.

Your first words, the very first point that you are going to make, must set you apart from IBM. If not, you are dead. Your technology will not set you apart and your company will not set you apart. As far as the audience is concerned, you are simply an alternative.

In the face of this challenge, EDS made the decision to change the presentation. They recognized that they had to do something entirely different from what the IBM team had done. If not, they would most likely lose the business. If they lost, they would lose both the one million cost-of-sales and the value of the contract.

The message that they delivered was that A.C. Nielsen did not need a technology provider. They did not need another box-shifting, technical relationship. Since A.C. Nielsen's survival was at stake, what they needed was a partner who would help them use IT as strategic differentiator.

EDS won the business and enjoyed many years of working with A.C. Nielsen.

The Co-Dependent Enterprise

Companies exist in a state of co-dependence with key suppliers, core competencies internally and customers. Companies are finding it necessary to rely on outside sources for increasing portions of their business processes, their value chain. Companies are finding it necessary to outsource critical corporate functions, even portions of their value chain previously considered "core".

In Japanese, these co-dependent relationships are called a "Keiretsu". A Keiretsu is a formal or informal group of companies who have chosen to exist in a state of mutual dependency, each relying on the other for significant portions of their value chain, even their core competencies.

The reason they do this is simple. The more core competencies that a company does for themselves, the more they must invest to develop and build their product. The more competencies they need internally, the higher the capital investment, diverting budget dollars away from their primary business and the creation of value for their customers. A.C. Nielsen did not want to be in the computer business.

"It's the Language"

The words which you select to communicate to customers and prospects set the tone for your relationship with them. Are you a vendor, or will you be a partner, a key supplier? How you express your value to them becomes the measure by which they will ultimately position you on their list of corporate priorities.

When you use product feature terms, they will send you to their own technologists, since they would be the ones who understand you. When you use benefit terminology, they send you to the management audience, since they are the ones chiefly concerned with the internal operational efficiencies of their company. However, when you use customer value terminology, they send you to the executive audience since they are the ones chiefly concerned with the creation of customer and shareholder value.

Whether you are in a prospecting mode or dealing with existing customers, you must use the appropriate language in such a way that they are open and willing to help you move your selling effort forward. Unfortunately, traditional approaches are not compelling. Traditional language is simply not effective anymore.

Feature, Benefit and Value

The concept of "Customer Value Orientation" is becoming the standard for salespeople engaged in prospecting and selling activities. The objective of these activities is to create interest and willingness on the part of a customer to invest their time with you, and ultimately to consider a purchase, and a relationship with you and your company.

The language that you use to describe your value to customers falls into three categories. Feature Oriented Statements are statements that use your product as the central theme. Benefit Oriented Statements are statements that explain the output of those features. Finally, Customer Value Oriented Statements are statements that refer to the financial impact of your offering. Each of these orientations is a legitimate approach to customers, but only with the appropriate audience.

Salespeople often revert to what they know best, their offering. Since they know a lot about their offering, they are most comfortable talking about their offering. This is entirely appropriate at the lower levels of an organization with the operational people who are themselves comfortable with this type of conversation.

The executive audience is usually not technically proficient, and if they are, technological minutiae are the least of their concerns. Rarely does an executive have the time or interest to keep up with the latest technological nuances in your industry. Using language that is mostly feature-oriented with the executive audience diminishes your value. They are not interested or concerned with the features of your product. Avoid using the wrong message with the wrong audience.

Feature Selling

Over the years, the perspective of salespeople migrated. It used to be enough for salespeople to talk about the wonderful features of their offering. In a feature statement, the focus is on the offering and the features of the offering. "It will do this; it has that many; it lasts this long and it will not ruin the carpet." The feature statement is all about the product.

As time went on, customers became suspicious of the escalating exaggerations of salespeople. Customers became more adept at leaving the conversation. They did not want to hear the pitch and they were not going to be sold anything. They would rather have root canal surgery than listen to one more second of a sales pitch. This kind of selling has become ineffective, even with the operational audience.

Benefit Selling

The next orientation looks at the customer's condition and seeks to connect empathetically with their problems. It is called Benefit Selling since you are referring to the benefits, the output, of the features.

The idea behind the orientation to Benefit Selling is that, if a salesperson can help a customer recognize a problem, they are initiating the customer's buying process. Instead of talking about the features of their offering, they are talking about the customer and their problems. The salesperson is making the customer aware that they can help them solve a problem, a problem they might not have known of otherwise. This is more compelling than a simple feature approach. Using the Benefit Selling approach with the right audience is sometimes still effective, but unfortunately, it is becoming less effective. As customers become more cognizant of this approach, they become desensitized. As more salespeople use this approach, customers become more suspicious, more skeptical and less receptive.

The CVO Approach

The next level of selling has taken the Benefit Selling approach one-step further. The Customer Value Oriented (CVO) approach in business-to-business selling is a disciplined approach focused on the customer's financial success. For example, "Our service platform will enable you to develop longer, more profitable relationships with your customers, increasing your profit margins" or, "Our experience in similar situations has helped our clients increase their average revenue per customer significantly."

The CVO approach talks about the financial impact on the customer's business. Their financial success is central to your concerns in this approach. The financial impact needs to be professional, credible and relevant to that particular customer. If they are not concerned about "average revenue per customer" then you are using the wrong financial measurement in your approach.

The CVO approach requires you to think in terms of the customer. It requires you to do your homework and understand the customer's industry and business. It requires that you spend more time researching before you ever make contact with the prospect. It requires that you know more about the sales situation than you need to know in the Feature or Benefit approaches.

The Numbers Game

Many sales managers believe that selling is a numbers game. If you make thirty calls, someone is going to say "Yes". There are managers that require salespeople to make fifty or more cold calls a day. This activity management approach to sales is valid in some markets and with certain types of offerings. Where the market is vast numbers of prospects and the offering is of less economic impact, activity management may be useful.

The CVO approach does not apply to markets of vast, undifferentiated customers. The CVO approach would not apply to a smaller value proposition. The CVO approach would not apply to the operational level.

Using the CVO approach is not a numbers game, or an issue of quantity. The CVO approach is an issue of quality. High-level, professional selling requires you to focus on the customer's business. You need to know what their business is about, how they differentiate themselves from their competitors, what their market share is and what markets they serve.

Before you ever make the initial call, you need to know what their earnings are, and what investment analysts think about their company and their industry. You need to know how other businesses in their industry measure success. You need to know what key measurements dominate their industry. High-level selling requires that you use different competencies.

Preparing for this kind of call can seem daunting, particularly at the beginning. If you know nothing about the industry where you are going to be calling, you need to do your research. If you know little about the company you will be calling, you need to do your research. If you know nothing about the job responsibilities of the person you will be calling, you need to do more research. However, as you become more aware of customer issues and different industries, the research will take less time.

Different industries and companies have different ways of measuring financial performance. Some companies might use a measurement as simple as sales, profit margins or number of customer orders. Most industries and companies have much more sophisticated ways of measuring their performance. For example, one key measurement in the retail-banking sector has been the average number of accounts per customer. Banks realized that their customers had many different types of banking relationships with many different institutions. Their customers had checking, savings, credit cards and mortgages. They had insurance and investment accounts as well. By increasing the average number of accounts per customer, banks would capture more of their customer's business. By increasing their average accounts per customer, they would enhance their total profitability.

You may think that all this research for one call is excessive. If you intend to call at a lower, operational position, all that homework would be unnecessary. However, if you intend to approach the prospect company at a higher, executive level, using the CVO approach, then all that research is not only necessary, it's vital to your success.

The Declaration of Value

The Declaration of Value is your opening statement to a prospect or a customer. It is the justification for the time you will be asking them to spend with you. It is used at the beginning of a conversation, a presentation or a proposal. The goal of the Declaration of Value is to create interest in developing a value-oriented relationship with you.

The Declaration of Value answers the following three questions in a single statement. First, why should the prospect or customer listen to you? Second, what is the business contribution you can provide? Finally, what is the financial measurement that your value proposition affects?

Your Credibility

The answer to the first question, "Why should the customer listen to you?" is your credibility and your experience in helping other businesses with similar problems. The experience that went into creating your offering or potential offering is one aspect of your credibility. Another aspect of your credibility is your experience in similar situations. If you lack such experience, it is acceptable to borrow the credibility of others in your organization, such as your manager or someone from the marketing organization.

The Business Contribution

The second question is "What is the business contribution you can provide?" The business contribution is the area of the customer's business that will benefit from your offering. It may be that they could improve customer satisfaction, or product development times. They may be better able to manage inventory or more efficiently use existing capital resources. Your answer is to identify a part of their internal operations that you can help them improve.

Financial Impact

The last question, "What is the financial measurement that your value proposition affects?" is the customer-relevant financial measurement that your offering will affect. You may be able to help them improve their profit margins or increase their sales. You may be able to help them increase market share, increase average accounts per customer or increase shareholder value. The answer to this question is a financial measurement that is meaningful to the customer.

Answering these three questions in a single sentence is your Declaration of Value, for that particular customer. You have done your research and taken the time to understand your value for that particular customer. If you get it right, you are connecting with this customer in a professional manner. You are connecting with the business issues and measurements that are meaningful to that customer.

Be careful. After using the CVO approach for a while, you might begin to generalize your Value Declaration to one or two basic statements. You cannot allow yourself to fall into the unfortunate habit of expedience when preparing for this type of call. You have only one chance to get through to that individual. You must genuinely set yourself apart from the rest of the world and compel that person to alter their plans and engage in conversation with you.

Ideal Outcome

The ideal outcome for your Value Declaration is not to take an order on the spot. Large, complex selling situations do not work that way. The ideal outcome from this approach would be to initiate a continuing Customer Value Oriented dialog centered on the creation of a unique Value Proposition. This Value Proposition is co-authored with the executive's organization, and is the result of your consultative, CVO approach. It is focused on the customer's financial results, not on the product set, or the services that you would like the customer to buy.

The theme of your sales campaign is beginning to sound like, "What you are not buying is a software platform or communication system. What you are buying is higher margins."

The purpose of Customer Value Orientation is to change the character of the dialog between you and your prospects and customers. Prospects and customers are tired of being pitched with the latest and greatest. They are tired of salespeople operating in sales mode. You will still go into sales mode, but only at the right time and with the permission of the customer. When customers recognize that you have done your research, that you are approaching them as a unique, one-of-a-kind entity, and you are genuinely interested in their success and their business issues, you begin to earn the right to a more privileged relationship.

Understanding Value

How many times have you watched a friend or family member purchase a "safe car" just when their first child arrives? Why do you suppose so many people's interest in safety seems to notch up two or three degrees when they become parents for the first time? It makes you wonder if the Volvo salesperson should be prospecting in the halls of the maternity ward.

In business, as in life, we are frequently interested in buying those things that help us handle risk. In business, there is a relationship between risk and value. For example, some companies buy only the latest and greatest technology while other companies are happy to use vintage equipment. Why does one company insist on the latest/greatest while another company does not? The reason is that one company feels that staying up with rapid technological change is central to their success and will spend more to support their belief. The other company sees technology as a less important factor in their strategy.

Companies go through many planning steps to create their corporate plans. They develop a corporate plan; they disseminate that plan to the organization; all parts of the organization translate that plan into local orders. In the plan, they are declaring the purpose and the direction of their company based on their existing and anticipated capital investments, their intellectual capital, their identified markets, their competition and their vision of the future.

At the heart of this planning activity is the desire to sell products or services to their identified markets at a price that results in profits. These profits must be greater than their operating costs plus their cost of capital. These profits are the fruit of the capitalist market system, creating some form of shareholder value.

Businesses do not have an inherent right to exist. In the absence of profits, a business will cease to exist. Looking back only ten or twenty years at the largest companies in the world, you would find names like Control Data, Digital Equipment, Wang Laboratories, Bethlehem Steel and Tandem Computers. All of these companies were large, successful companies with impressive pedigrees and impressive offerings. Today, they are all but gone.

Even the largest companies are not immune to the ebb and flow of competition. Companies like Polaroid, Eastman Kodak, and Xerox, genuine blue chip companies, are currently trying to reinvent themselves into more relevant value providers. Even though Microsoft is dominant in many of their markets, they still live in a constant state of high-paranoia to competitive threats. Bill Gates, during the anti-trust trial, said that Microsoft is within two years of going out of business unless they continue to innovate and create value for their customers.

Shareholder versus Customer Value

There was a reversal in thinking during the 1990's Internet boom. Business people created companies with new business models in order to create shareholder value as their first priority, as opposed to creating customer value. They identified markets, built a business plan and then, based on the insane growth forecasts in the utilization of the internet, they were able to command market capitalizations that had little to do with their financial results. At the beginning of 2000, Amazon's stock market valuation exceeded the combined market value of the three major North American airlines, Delta, American and United.

We can easily recognize the folly of the extreme speculation of the stock market in hindsight, but at the time, the creation of shareholder value and wealth were the paramount concerns in those companies. We would see companies, with little more than a business plan, command market capitalizations of over a billion dollars. The presumption was that these companies would eventually create enough value for their customers to justify those insane market capitalizations. We all seemed to forget the basic tenet of business; in the absence of the creation of customer value, shareholder wealth will not endure.

Survival

The over-riding priority of any company is to survive. In order to survive, they must create some form of value for their customers. While a well-established company may not be facing their own extinction daily, if things got bad enough, their primary goal would soon become survival.

Your job, as a high-level salesperson, is to understand the risks and the challenges faced by your customers. Your job is to create value propositions that relate directly to those risks. The relationship of risk and value will help you create compelling reasons for customers to do business with you.

Risk and Value Profile

Understanding where your customers face risk will make the creation of value easier and more relevant for you. The creation of value in the absence of risk is not meaningful. The creation of value where the customer does not perceive risk leaves your offering as nice-to-have but not mandatory.

In business, there are two categories of risk. There are external risks that are outside the immediate control of a company and internal risks that are inside the control of a company. External risks are part of the economic landscape and systemic in nature. Internal risks are risks that a company is in a position to control. An internal risk is one of execution, expense control, revenue creation; something that is within the internal scope of a company's operation.

External Business Risks

There are three categories of External Business Risks: Operating Cost Risks, Financial Market Risks and Economic Risks.

Operating Cost Risks

Operating Cost Risks are risks that can affect a company's cost-of-goods-sold. These include raw materials, labor costs, legislated costs, and other operating expenditures involved in producing a product.

An example of Operating Cost Risks would be the relationship between coffee beans and Starbucks Coffee. If there were a freeze in the coffee growing regions of the world, coffee bean prices would rise on the open market. In order for Starbucks to make your favorite cup of coffee, they must buy, no matter the cost, the right coffee beans. They may be able to continue using their existing inventory, but eventually they would have to replace those beans at the higher prices or stop selling coffee. Starbucks does not control the cost of their raw material. Starbucks' operating costs are at risk.

In contrast to Starbucks is Wrigley's Gum. This is a very old company that has for many years controlled their entire value chain from raw materials all the way through their manufacturing process and out to their distributors. They own the sources of their raw materials (a closely guarded company secret) by owning the plantations in Central and South America where the chicle is grown. Many years ago, Wrigley's chose to control all of the aspects of their production. They are vertically integrated. Their operating cost risk, therefore, is different from Starbucks. They still have risk, but it is of a distinctly different nature.

Looking at a company's financial report, the term to look for is operating costs. Operating costs are expressed as a percentage of sales. For example, if operating costs are 64%, then company spends 64 cents of every dollar on operating costs or cost of goods sold. They would also have operating profits of 36%, the reciprocal of 64%.

In addition to knowing what a customer's operating costs are, it is interesting to compare their costs against other companies' costs in their industry. How one company compares to another in the same industry is important for you to know. If their cost ratios are better or worse than their competitors, you might be able to identify areas of opportunity for the creation of value.

Microsoft is an interesting company in many ways, not the least of which is their operating expenses. Microsoft, as an integral part of their operating philosophy, decided that they are a software development company, interested only in creating, marketing and selling software to mass markets worldwide. Because of their philosophy, they have consistently outsourced every non-essential aspect of their operations. They do not own replication equipment to manufacture their software; it is outsourced. When they decided to come out with their own game box, the "X Box", they did not build factories and manufacturing processes. They chose instead to outsource to contract manufacturers.

Because of this philosophy, Microsoft's operating costs are among the lowest in the world. This allows them to focus their resources on what they feel they do best. Because of Microsoft's philosophy, the type of value that they are concerned with is different from other companies. This difference influences the kind of value that would interest them. The salesperson who is able to recognize this is able to create a Value Proposition directly applicable to their financial interests.

Years ago, a consulting company was interested in selling a new service to Microsoft. In spite of some very senior relationships between the companies, the sales effort stalled. The new service they were attempting to sell to Microsoft was a cost recovery service where the consulting company would find areas for cost reduction. They were able to reduce costs and even recover significant amounts of money for their other clients.

The reason their sales effort stalled was that cost reduction did not represent a significant risk to Microsoft. Operating expenses were well under control and of little or no concern to Microsoft.

Financial Market Risks

The next category of external risk is those risks associated with capital formation and the public financial markets. Included in this category would be stock market valuations, interest rates and foreign exchange rates. When companies borrow money or have excess cash, they are subject to whatever current pricing is available on the open market. When companies seek to raise equity capital by selling their stock to the public with an IPO or a secondary offering, they are subject to the general valuation levels of the stock market at that moment in time. If they invest in other public companies with their excess cash, they are also subject to fluctuating stock market valuations. If they are a multi-national company doing business in multiple currencies, they are subject to the vagaries of the currency markets.

All of these financial risks are outside the direct control of a company. They cannot directly control these risks. There are, of course, sophisticated financial strategies that companies employ to mitigate or hedge these financial risks using futures, options and forward contracts. These insurance hedge programs allow companies to manage the financial risks they face. However, outright, direct control is not an outcome of these hedging programs.

Economic Risks

The last category of external risk is economic risk. The world economies grow and contract. Every company is subject to this backdrop of economic activity from a macroeconomic and a microeconomic perspective. At the microeconomic level, companies are involved in industries that have their own relevance to the macro economy, and will grow and or contract accordingly.

An example of microeconomic contraction was seen in the auto parts aftermarket of the last ten years. As the lifespan of the average automobile part has gone from five or seven years, to ten plus years due to quality initiatives in the auto industry, the replacement cycle of the aftermarket has caused a protracted decline in sales.

Another example of microeconomic activity is evident in the cell phone industry in major Latin American markets. The cell phone market in Latin America has seen explosive growth for many years in a row, in spite of economic contractions. The reason is unique. In Latin America, cell phones are an attractive alternative to hard wire telephones. In some of these countries, it could take years for the local phone company to install a hard wire phone. However, customers can purchase a cell phone and use it within minutes.

In a macroeconomic sense, all companies great and small live inside the global market system. If the system is healthy and growing, companies should grow with the general health of the world economy. How companies perform in relation to their industry and in relation to the world economy should give you an indication as to how your customer might perceive his risks. It could help you build a relevant value proposition for them.

Compare your customer's growth with their industry. Are they in line, ahead or behind? Do they outperform or under perform compared to their competitors? Are they gaining market share or losing market share? These are important factors for you to know.

Internal Business Risks

Internal business risks fall into three categories: Expense Control, Investment Risk and Revenue Risk.

Expense Control

The first level of internal business risk is Expense Control, to spend or not to spend. If they decide to spend, then what do they buy and why do they buy it? Controlling expenses is a central theme in many companies, one familiar to most salespeople. When a customer is forcing you to negotiate a lower price, they are dealing with the fundamental economic issues of making finite resources go farther, more bang for the buck.

There is a difference between these expenses, the internal risk of expense control and the cost category previously defined as cost of goods sold or operating costs. The difference is that the internal expense control expenditures are paid from the operating profit of a company. These expenses are discretionary. Companies can spend this money any way they see fit. The types of expenditures that are a part of this category are things like marketing programs, advertising, research and development, building maintenance, SG&A, to name only a few.

Helping customers control or reduce expenses is a common value proposition that can be very appealing to your customers.

Investment Risk

The next internal business risk category is Investment Risk. Companies spend enormous sums of money for capital equipment that needs to meet some minimum level of performance. When a company buys a robotic manufacturing system, for example, some level of Return on Investment (ROI) is necessary to justify the investment. As salespeople, you can develop value propositions based on improving their investment return for a proposed purchase.

Revenue Risk

The last area of internal business risk is revenue risk. The search for, and the exploitation of revenue streams, is central to any company. In order for companies to create or sustain revenue streams, they must create a product or a service that is valuable to a customer or a market segment. As high-level salespeople, you can help your customer build value propositions around new or existing forms of revenue.

Each of these internal business risks is controllable and represents an opportunity for you to create value.

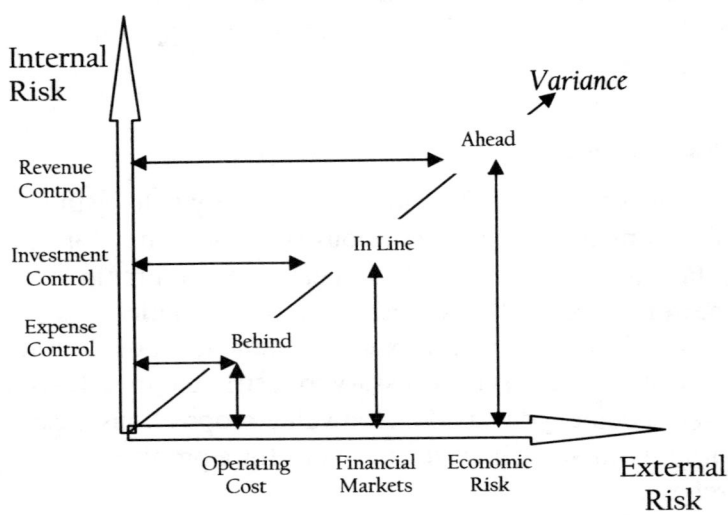

Comparing Internal and External Business Risks

The first internal business risk is expense control and the first external business risk is operating cost. Expense control is paid from a company's operating profit. Operating profit is the money left over after the operating costs, costs of goods sold, are paid.

By accounting rules, the money customers pay you affects either operating costs or their operating profit. In operating costs, the money they pay you is recognized as part of their raw materials cost, their cost of goods sold. This is a cost they hope to pass on to their customers. On the other hand, if the money they pay you affects operating profits, then this discretionary expenditure will affect the profits they report to their shareholders.

In competitive markets, companies frequently compete on price. Dropping prices will lower a company's operating profits. As profits fall, companies have less money to spend on your services. They will seek ways to extend their limited resources by forcing their own suppliers to drop their prices. They push you to drop your prices. They will lead you to believe that their only motivation for buying is price. However, that is not the reason they do business with you.

The reason they buy is motivated by the other risk categories. Their motivation might be a financial return, a business case argument. Their motivation might be a revenue motivation seeking opportunities to enhance existing revenue streams or develop new ones. Externally, they may be trying to better manage or reduce their exposure to financial market fluctuations. Their motivation may be declining performance in relationship to their competitors.

Your customer's buying motivation is never your price. They ask for price concessions from you, and may even buy from someone else if they are less expensive. However, fundamentally, their motivation is not price. It is motivated by something else in their risk profile.

You need to be aware of the risk factors that are driving your customer's decision process. You need to be aware of the differences between your customer and other companies in their industry. How do they compare to their competitors? Are they ahead, in line with, or behind other companies in their market? If they were ahead, what kind of value proposition would be most compelling to them? If they were behind, what kind of value proposition would be most compelling to them? Just as with Microsoft's lack of interest in the consulting company's new offering, the type of value that you need to represent to a prospect or a customer needs to be relevant to their situation, their market position.

When you are able to recognize these things, you are able to create a value proposition that is pertinent to your customer. It takes a good deal more research, but this level of insight gives you a much greater ability to Create Demand. The absence of this insight will leave you in vendor status.

Key Business Drivers

Companies operate in response to their own planning process and to external market pressures. They operate under the force of Key Business Drivers or "KBD's". KBD's are company priorities shaped by the success or failure of their business plan in the presence of market pressure. Few companies can afford to wait until their next formal planning session to make adjustments or decisions that affect their business plans. Very often, companies have an identified list of KBD's.

High-level selling requires you to understand and support your customer's KBD's. You may even play a central role in the identification of a KBD. This high-level, consultative role creates demand for your offering. It happens if you clearly understand your customer's risk/value profile as well as their KBD's.

A Fortune 500 company invited a salesperson to participate in competition for a training contract. The customer had a long history of predatory buying, negotiating large concessions from their major suppliers. The customer took great pride in the concessions they extracted, heralding great victories in their company's newspaper.

Initially, the customer persecuted the salesperson, asking for projects to prove that their training worked - an expensive project for the salesperson. The customer called meetings with useless agendas on a whim, causing the salesperson to have to fly to the meetings, a costly proposition. However, the salesperson took time to do research about the customer. The salesperson found the motivation behind the training initiative. The salesperson discovered that the customer's gross profit margin had shrunk from 42% to 28% in the previous five years. They needed those profits to fund their aggressive growth initiative into foreign markets.

Using this insight, the salesperson was able to connect with the customer's real problem, shrinking margins. The value proposition migrated from a price/scope-of-service type of dialog to a value-oriented dialog focusing on improving margins. As the focus of the dialog shifted away from price toward margins, the predatory buying practices abated. The customer became more cooperative, assisting the salesperson in the development of the value proposition.

By understanding the KBD's and understanding the potential value for the customer, the salesperson gained a competitive advantage over the other training companies vying for the business. It also increased his access to senior executives. He gained access to several VP's and had a monthly meeting with the CEO.

By connecting the KBD's to the potential value of the training initiative, the scope of the project increased from a $250,000 intervention to a $1.2 million engagement. The scope increased from classroom only to consulting and development work. The predator had become a cooperative colleague, addressing the real issues facing their company.

When your offering becomes closely associated with a high-priority KBD, the momentum created for your selling effort can be tremendous. Creating this association and helping the customer prioritize the KBD is a critical component of Creating Demand.

The Value Chain

A company's internal processes that convert a raw material into a finished good are referred to as a Value Chain. The Value Chain is divided into three groups of process steps – Supply Side, Internal Operations and Demand Side Processes. The supply side of the value chain is the sourcing of the required materials, parts, and services that a company must purchase in order to supply the internal business processes that will convert those materials into a marketable product. The internal operational processes are the product creation and support aspects of the value chain. These are typically the core competencies of an organization. On the demand side are the customers of the value chain, the business process steps directed toward the markets and the customers.

At the highest levels of selling, you can have a dramatic impact on the way your customer does business. You can help the customer improve performance by redesigning aspects of their value chain.

It was not that long ago that the environmental control, heating and air conditioning, of large buildings was a mundane business. Salespeople sold to the maintenance manager, a relatively low-level position, who made purchasing decisions.

For a maintenance manager, a building's environment is a high priority. They are caught between the demands for a comfortable environment and maintenance of the system. The maintenance manager is happiest when the system functions without incident. The building ownership and senior managers grapple with energy costs, which in some large buildings run into the millions.

Most of the salespeople in this market had been finding it increasingly difficult to compete for their $10-15 thousand average sale, running into the maintenance manager's need for lower price and reliability and a competitor's willingness to drop prices. Where there had been long-term relationships between the maintenance manager and a salesperson, increasingly, these good relationships were being lost to lower prices. Johnson Controls and Honeywell salespeople frequently found themselves forced into deep price discounting or faced the prospect of losing the business altogether.

The idea that changed the industry was to approach the market from an entirely different angle, to change the rules of the game. The idea was that instead of approaching the maintenance managers and hoping for a $10-15 thousand sale, why not move toward a new audience with an entirely different value proposition?

The concept they introduced was to sell a total environment. No energy cost, no maintenance headaches, no hassle. The building owners would outsource their building's environment to Johnson Controls and later Honeywell, for a flat fixed annual price. The cost of the contract would usually be less than what they had previously spent on their environment. So, instead of selling a price-competitive piece of capital equipment for $10-15 thousand, salespeople found themselves selling service contracts for millions of dollars. The new value proposition was so compelling that large pieces of significant business shifted away from Honeywell.

What happened in this example was the realization that the customer was managing portions of their own Value Chain that the provider could handle better. They were managing heating and air conditioning systems that were not a central part of their ongoing business. It required a different kind of relationship between supplier and buyer, involving more trust and more access. However, once the two sides realized the potential, they quickly adjusted to the new relationship. Instead of being outside trying to get in, the salespeople had keys to the buildings and total access.

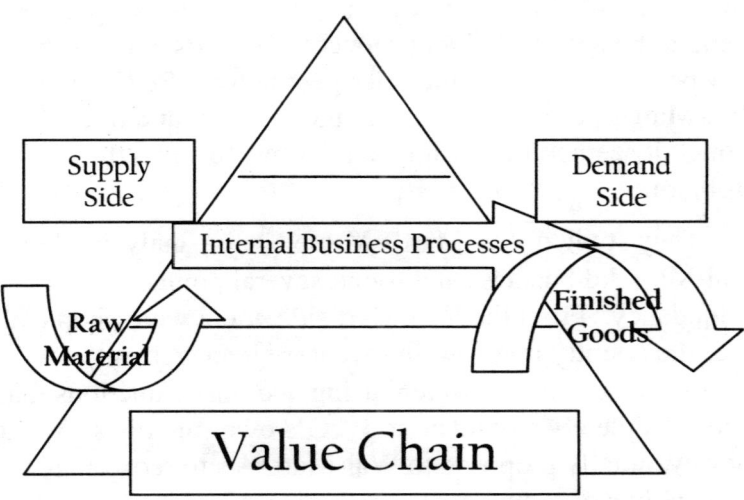

Connecting to the Value Chain

Creating customer value involves your ability to identify and articulate your customer's risk/value profile, KBD's and the potential impact of those on their Value Chain. Those external forces shaping your customer's business creates opportunity for you, opportunity to connect to your customer's value chain in a meaningful, important way. This could make your offering a mandatory purchase.

When you understand how you connect or could potentially connect to your customer's Value Chain, you can help them enhance, improve, even revolutionize the way they do business.

Some years ago, Proctor and Gamble wanted to do business with Wal-Mart. While they had done business in the past, due to some new policies and some aggressive pricing by P&G's competition, they faced elimination as a supplier to Wal-Mart. P&G was not, by their own policies, going to be able to deliver product to Wal-Mart under the new policies. Some of the sales people from P&G obtained Wal-Mart's permission to study the problem and try, though it seemed impossible at the time, to solve the problem.

They studied Wal-Mart's Value Chain, analyzing how Wal-Mart did business and found several points of redundancy. From the Wal-Mart side, there were people all over the country involved in inventory management, payables, receivables, warehousing and other functions that were completely redundant to P&G's own functions. What they eventually proposed to Wal-Mart was to reorganize those points of redundancy, combining the offsetting functions into more efficient, automated processes. This would require Wal-Mart to share information with P&G in a non-traditional way, giving P&G access to sensitive information. This created tremendous cost savings between the two companies and allowed for a better price point from P&G. By combining Wal-Mart's Value Chain with P&G's into a closer, more integrated relationship, P&G won back the business.

The Buying Process

In addition to considering your customer's risk value profile, their KBD's and their Value Chain, it is important to understand where your customer is in their Buying Process. The buying process is the steps that companies go through to arrive at a buying decision.

Through the buying process, a company is able to determine how a proposed purchase connects to their corporate plan, whether they should buy it or build it, filtering out the choices and finally arriving at the buying point. The buying process should also include, in some way, the post-implementation evaluation as to whether or not the purchase delivered the intended value and whether the corporate plan should be changed to accommodate the delivery, or lack of delivery, of the intended value.

Your customers do not buy in the absence of motivation. Usually, there are specific reasons supporting buying decisions. If a company has a long history of buying a particular product or raw material, they will not frequently return to the primary initiatives. They may challenge the supplier on price and seek alternatives, but in the case of a history of buying, customers will infrequently go back to the specific reasoning for the purchase.

Customers, at one time or another, typically follow steps in reaching a buying decision. The first step is the Corporate Plan. This is the executive level planning session. The senior people come together to define the direction and shape of the future of their organization. They try to come to some definition of their company's specific requirements and solutions in the context of their market. At this point, they cannot articulate what they will need to buy. However, it is possible to trace the genesis for buying decisions to the corporate plan.

Corporate Initiatives is the next step in the buying process. Initiatives are the marching orders the executives communicate to their organization. They serve a company as a priority-setting tool. They may call them goals, visions, critical success factors, even KBD's. The genesis for a corporate initiative is the identification of a problem or an opportunity the senior managers wish to pursue. From increasing environmental awareness programs to finding and entering new markets, from hiring more salespeople to increasing employee satisfaction and retention, the high-level corporate initiatives indicate to a whole company what the direction of the enterprise will be. At this level, there is still no clearly defined way of going in those directions, the "how" of moving in those directions. A corporate initiative only indicates that the company is moving in a particular direction.

The next step in the buying process is alternative identification and analysis. This is the "how" to move in a given direction and requires careful thought and analysis. Alternative identification and analysis is the thinking that goes between concept and action. In order to move in a direction, they need to decide if it is better to build it themselves, buy it from known suppliers or acquire it by buying another company. What are the financial returns of each of these alternatives? Which alternative available best serves the long-term direction of the company? What providers can they identify? Important decisions are going to be made in alternative identification and analysis.

Create Demand

The short list is the list of finalists in the buying process. The finalists will be closely scrutinized. They will be asked to prove concepts and demo their wares. They are in the final showdown. In this late stage of the buying process, customers will begin negotiating price, scope and levels of service and other terms they might be seeking.

Based on the competition between the short list finalists, the customer will select their final option. The winner is declared and implementation dates and time schedules are established. If the customer is fully prepared for the purchase and the implementation, the finalist may find that their value is limited to product or service only. They will deliver the product or the service and no further intervention will be required. However, if the customer is relatively unprepared for the purchase, the type of value that the finalist could represent may be greater.

The next step in the buying process is the implementation of the purchase. Even though this is post-purchase, to the customer it is not the end of their buying process. At this point, the traditional Phase II salesperson will usually disappear from the customer environment. Sometimes they are replaced by engineers or other post-sales specialists. However, operating as a high-level salesperson requires you to remain as a voice of the customer within your organization and as a confidence builder for the customer.

The last step in the customer's buying process is results analysis. Even though the purchase was made months before, the high-level salesperson can become a part of the customer's analysis of the value that the purchase has returned. Has your offering delivered the kind of value that was promised? Has it met the customer's expectations of performance?

If you are not a part of this analysis, one of several things could happen. First, your offering delivers the expected returns, but you are unaware. Next, your offering fails to deliver the expected returns and you are unaware. If you are not part of the analysis, you would have no way of receiving appropriate credit for the implementation, or you would have no way of knowing that you have a problem.

Conversely, if you are a part of the analysis of the implemented platform, you will be aware of the success or failure of the implementation. This puts you in a position to correct a problem, if one exists, further enhancing your value. This would also put you in a position to receive credit for meeting or exceeding the buying expectations of the customer.

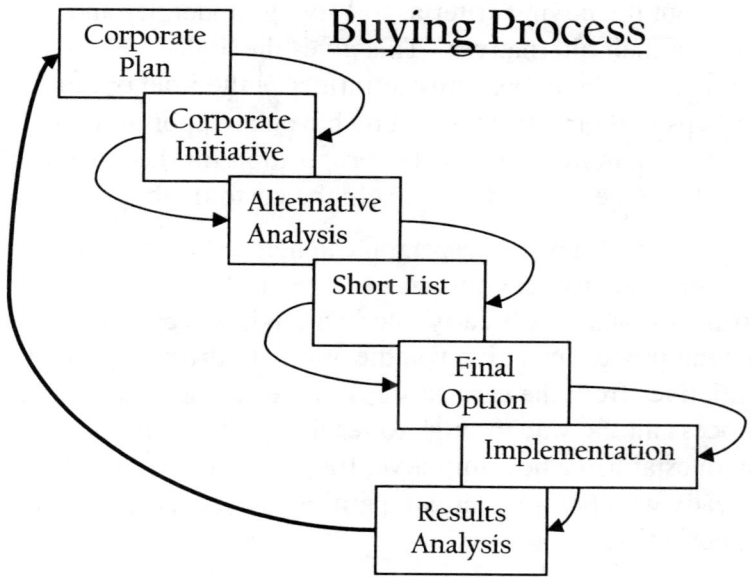

Buying Process

It is important for you to recognize where your customers are in their buying process. For example, if they are well advanced in the buying process, the opportunity for you to create a unique, value oriented value proposition may require a different kind of selling strategy on your part. If the customer is advanced in the buying process, they are comfortable with the decisions they have already made. Momentum has already been created for a particular decision and the decision-making responsibility has been handed over to operational level people. The operational level people have been tasked to get it done and are powerful enough to select the supplier, but not to change the buying criteria in any significant way.

If the customer is not advanced in their buying process, this will also influence your selling strategy. At the earlier points of the buying process, the customer is still trying to work out the buying criteria, still trying to identify and analyze their alternatives. This gives the high-level salesperson the opportunity to influence the final option, perhaps to their advantage. You have the opportunity to establish a more critical value proposition for the customer. You have the opportunity to help the customer buy.

The high-level salesperson can help the customer establish a corporate initiative or even influence their corporate plan. This early intervention in the customer's buying process can give you the ability to drive important initiatives from the earliest steps of the customer's buying process all the way through to results analysis. If you help them establish a new initiative, frequently you may have already won before your competition is even aware of the opportunity.

Value Based Pricing

A critical part of your job in high-level selling is to understand how much your value proposition is worth to your customer. If you are unaware of the financial impact of your offering, you run the risk of either asking too much in your pricing or, just as importantly, not asking enough.

If the financial return is less than your price, the customer will balk, and rightfully so. However, will the customer be aware of the return on the investment they made with you? They should, and if they do not, they will eventually work it out. Especially in large offerings and complex purchases, (the province of a high-level salesperson), the customer will formulate an opinion as to the value of your offering. They may calculate the actual return on investment or they may assume a return on investment. They may want to work out the financial impact before they purchase, in which case your close participation is not only warranted, it is healthy. They may work out the return on the investment after the purchase, depending on the types of financial analysis they use. In any case, you should never expect them to pay you more than what they expect to make on the purchase.

Traditional price strategies will use different concepts to establish an offering price. The cost/plus price model is where a company works out their cost of producing the offering and then adds a fair return. The fair return is the target profit margin the company seeks. Another price strategy is the good-better-best price strategy, where an offering is developed toward specific price targets. You can find cars, for example, built to satisfy customers with different price requirements. Another price strategy is street price, where the market has determined through multiple offerings, what a product is worth. In this case, the company is challenged to create ways of producing the product profitably at street price.

Consider the price strategies employed by consulting firms. Consulting companies are notoriously expensive, sometimes charging millions for what amounts to a single document. The cost of producing the document is minuscule compared to the price they charge. How can these companies charge these prices and why is it that customers pay?

Customers pay these prices for a myriad of justifiable reasons. They may feel that their own thinking is not clear enough for them to fashion their own plan for their future. They may feel that they need outside help to define their IT strategy, for example. They need outside help to know what "best-of-breed" companies are doing with their strategies. Whatever the reason, the consulting business has been a growth industry for years, so somebody is willing to pay those prices.

Consulting firms can charge astronomical prices because of the potential value of their recommendations. Their price strategy is based on the value that would be created if the customer implemented their recommendations. They base their prices on the value that they create for their customers and not on the cost involved in producing their product.

If the financial return for the customer is much greater than the price you are asking, then you should consider a value based price rather than a more traditional cost-plus pricing model. Sometimes, even when the customer is aware of your internal cost of producing your offering, it is acceptable and correct to expect much higher prices and margins. Nothing could be more tragic than selling an offering for a price that is too low relative to what a customer could be willing to pay. It is a case of leaving money on the table. Your total value to a customer is greater than your price; they would be happy to pay you more for everything you do for them, but because you are unaware of your value to them, you fail to recognize the opportunity.

The Co-Authored Value Proposition

The purpose of the CVO approach is to change the character and nature of the dialog between you and your customer. If you are engaged with your customers in a conversation about their markets and their financial returns, you have succeeded in changing your status from vendor to partner. The CVO approach is a powerful way of cementing relationships with your customers.

The CVO dialog is designed to develop, in conjunction with your customer, a co-authored value proposition. They are involved in the research and analysis that supports the value proposition. They will develop a sense of ownership and responsibility in the success of the value proposition. They will have less time or interest in talking to your competitor when they are engaged with you in the development of a value proposition.

Do not publish a value proposition unless the customer has participated in the development of the value proposition. If you develop a value proposition in the absence of customer input and show it to the customer, their reaction may be the opposite of what you want. Instead of appreciating the value proposition, they might actively engage in subterfuge to see to its demise since it might reflect poorly on them. By presenting a value proposition that is not developed in concert with the customer, you run the risk of being completely incorrect, ruining your credibility. Restoring credibility is difficult, if not impossible.

Even if you do not have the cooperation of the customer in the development of the value proposition, it can be a valuable exercise. You would use it to determine how much you are worth to them in financial terms. However, do not show it to the customer.

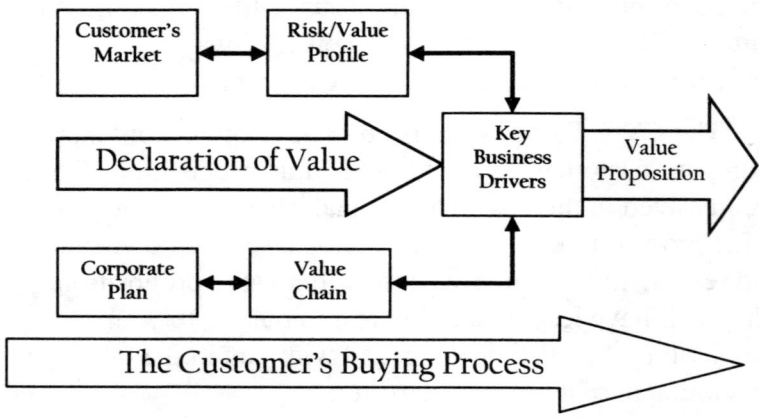

Customer Value Orientation

Areas of Development

Reflecting back on the customer's risk/value profile, you will find that your value proposition will center around three distinct areas of customer concern. Each of these relates directly to the customer's internal business risks: Expense value propositions, Investment/Financial value propositions and Revenue value propositions.

Expense or Price Based Value Propositions

Nothing could be more degrading to a high-level salesperson attempting to use the CVO approach than, at the end of it all the customer says, "So, tell me, what you can do for me on the price?" It is true that price can still be an issue all too often, but when you have established a unique value proposition and the customer still wants to nick you on price, it can be very disappointing.

The lowest form of value proposition that any salesperson can represent to their customer is a discounted price. Lowering your price in front of the customer to a high-level salesperson is failure; failure to establish a value proposition compelling enough to remove price as a buying issue. You know that your company cannot remain profitable if your prices keep dropping, and you know that if you drop your price too often the customer will come to expect further concessions. If the cycle continues, your company will have to adjust internally to remain economically viable, and invariably, one of the places to cut back is in the sales force, cutting resources, support and eventually headcount.

Competing on price, unfortunately, is all too common in many markets. It is, nonetheless a value proposition, though the least desirable.

In commoditized markets when you are selling to well-informed, self-reliant customers, they are able to force price concessions from suppliers, even their preferred supplier, because they do not need anything but product. They can handle the rest. The well-informed customer is able to unbundle the offering, stripping out the higher margin parts, leaving the salesperson with only the low margin business. Establishing a unique value proposition to this customer can be very difficult.

It may be possible to establish a higher-level value proposition with the executive audience, even for a commoditized offering. Unfortunately, already commoditized offerings are of little or no interest to executives. They long ago delegated the responsibility for this type of purchase to others in their company. The decision-maker will typically be an operational level person or a person from the purchasing department.

The operational level audience will have little interest in a business related value proposition. They do not have responsibility for investment returns or revenue generation. The CVO approach to the operational level would not impress or persuade.

One option in a commoditized market is to wrap the offering into larger, more complex, solution-oriented packages. Instead of selling the box, create offerings that would integrate the box and all the related components into one complete, plug-and-play solution. Many industries have gone through the box-to-solution migration over the

...om, computing and even service

...n as opposed to the box is a
...a commoditizing product or service.
...ation adds complexity to the
...have an even larger grasp on their
...his box-to-solution migration also
...y from the operations level buyer.
...lution set with the customer, you
...to a higher-level audience.

Investment Value Propositions

Building your value proposition around a financial result can be very compelling to your customer, especially with the higher-level audiences, the management level or the executive level. In this kind of value proposition, you are seeking to associate your offering as being a more compelling investment opportunity than your competitors.

If you have some empirical study demonstrating that your offering will pay for itself in a shorter period of time than your competitor's, you will want to use it to help the customer develop a value proposition.

Many marketing organizations have developed sales tools that use this type of financial comparison. They can be effective ways for salespeople to start a more value-oriented dialog with the higher levels. However, as a stand alone tool, these instruments frequently amount to little more than a door opener. Your competitor probably has a similar tool that will show their offering more compelling than yours.

One of the more common financial arguments that companies use is a "Total Cost of Ownership" or "TCO" study. While this and other similar instruments are valuable, they should only be used to initiate a financially oriented dialog with your customer. Use it to open doors that you might not have otherwise knocked on. Use it to change the character of the dialog, moving away from the "me and my stuff" conversation toward a genuinely professional, consultative approach.

In many high-level sales campaigns, the CFO is going to require the buying process to produce a financial model before ever signing off on the purchase. It is better for you to be involved with the financial analysis aspects of the buying process than to leave the buyers alone, or worse, to leave the buyers working with your competitor.

A large Fortune 500 company was contemplating the purchase of $3 million dollars in laptop computers. They solicited proposals from IBM, Compaq, Dell and a couple of local re-sellers. They went through the various buying steps, interviewing the vendors, analyzing the products and a rudimentary financial step to determine which vendor to buy from and whether to lease the equipment or buy it. In the end, the winning team informed of their success was told to come by the office the next Tuesday to sign the contracts.

During the meeting, they were interrupted by the CFO, who came in for only a few seconds with some additional instructions, "Congratulations, folks. However, I need just one more thing before I write the check. I need to show the Board an 18% ROI. That is the hurdle rate for new capital spending. Get me that figure and I'll sign the check." Since the buyers had never built an ROI for laptops before,

Create Demand

it seemed logical that the sales team should do the work; after all, they have the studies to develop the financial model. They agreed to do the ROI and to return it by the end of the week. After two weeks, they had yet to respond.

After chasing down the salesperson, the key buyer found out the truth. The problem was not with developing an ROI of 18%, the problem was developing an ROI at all. The sellers did not know how, and they were too busy to learn. They delegated the task to their marketing people, but they were too busy, too. The sale of $3 million represented nearly half of the sales team's quota, but they were too busy to help. In the end, the buyers were required to use their own talents to develop the ROI, and sell it to the CFO. The sellers still won the business, but they were never invited back.

For some of you, it might be daunting to work with financial models and analyze ROI, EBITDA, Payback Periods, EVA or the myriad other financial measurements that businesses use. After all, isn't it your job to sell and someone else's to do the financial drudgery?

As high-level professional salespeople, you are responsible for all of these things, even the financial modeling. It is your job to understand the financial aspects of your offering, and it is your job to help your customer develop their own financial model.

Revenue Value Propositions

Business is about the cultivation and exploitation of profitable revenue streams. Market opportunities are identified and offerings are created to exploit them. Companies spend literally billions of dollars every year to find and develop new sources of revenue. No revenue source is permanent. Sources of revenue are created, marketed, customers are acquired and eventually the product's life cycle ends. That is, it will reach maturity, level off and eventually decline, just to be replaced by something new and improved.

Have you ever gone to an antique store or flea market and noticed how many formerly well-known brands have become collectibles? There are people who now pay a lot of money for the packages of those defunct brands. Some companies, that existed years ago, do not exist today because they were unable to find new sources of revenue. Some companies that exist today will not exist tomorrow because they will be unable to find new sources of revenue; their existing offering's life cycle will expire.

If you are able to create a value proposition built around helping customers develop new sources of revenue, or if you can re-invigorate and sustain existing ones, you are developing one of the most powerful value propositions possible. In this type of relationship, your presence becomes an integral part of the customer's lifeblood, their revenue streams, and with it, some measure of competitive immunity.

Summary

Creating Demand is an essential part of high-level selling. It entails your ability to engage the customer in ways that exclude your offering or your technology. Your aim is to change the character of the dialog, focusing on the customer's business issues. You are directing the conversation to areas of concern more compelling to the customer.

It is your ability to act in a consultative way, resisting your natural desire to talk about your stuff. It involves non-traditional selling competencies. The competencies you need are business acumen, financial sophistication, research and analysis.

Your ability to use these competencies with the right audiences will help you overcome competitive threats. Creating Demand will help you establish a long-term, value oriented relationship with your customers. It has nothing to do with your offering, your price or the name of your company. It has everything to do with your Sales Excellence.

Pursue Opportunity

When the competitive sales situation presents itself, salespeople need to be able to build effective strategies to defeat their competition. They need to be able to execute the defensive countermeasures that disable their competitor. They need to be able to recognize when they should compete and when it would be best not to compete.

Introduction to Strategic Planning

Most people are, in their own way and to varying degrees, strategists. They will apply strategic thinking to the task ahead. They will define the priorities of a project so that they will do the various tasks required in the most efficient fashion. They think of the approach they should use in order to accomplish almost everything in life. Familiar tasks may no longer require the same amount of thought since by experience they know what the task requires. In facing a new task, they might look to those who have experience for insight to complete the task with minimum cost and the greatest likelihood of success.

Even though most people think strategically, very few people understand the concept of strategy, and fewer still can build a meaningful strategy that could be used by a group of people.

Building a strategic plan is designing the conditions necessary for the greatest probability of success. Strategic planning is the activity of putting into place a specific pathway toward a particular objective, goal or outcome. A specific pathway refers to the approach to accomplish the desired outcome.

In history, there are literally millions of examples of effective strategy. Naval history is full of examples in which a smaller fleet was able to decimate a larger well-armed fleet using their unique strengths and capitalizing on the weaknesses of their opponent. In the movie "Braveheart", Mel Gibson, creating a new strategy and using creative tactics and artful troop movements, was able to defeat (ostensibly for the first time in history) a horse-mounted assault.

There are many other examples where a flawed strategy brought about miserable and tragic defeat. When Napoleon tried to capture Russia by moving across the vast European continent, the entire affair (due to miscalculations by his military planners) was doomed from the beginning.

As they moved east from Paris on their march toward Moscow, they had not calculated the necessary support to provide their troops with food and arms. The farther they moved from Paris, the more difficult their task became. The Russian strategy, in response to the advancing army, was to hit and run, strike and retreat. As they retreated after every strike, they burned and destroyed the crops and livestock, a move that history now calls scorched earth. By doing this, they accomplished two things. They slowed the advance of the French and they eliminated their ability to feed themselves on the local food sources.

What Napoleon and his military planners failed to do was to calculate the Russians' strategy. They did not expect them to destroy their own resources. The planners expected to be able to use resources they would capture on their journey to Moscow. However, the Russians destroyed everything that might be useful to the French prior to their many retreats, an act that brought great hardship to their own people as well as to the French.

Finally, as winter set in, the French troops were too weak, too tired and improperly equipped to be able to advance. As they began the long retreat back to Paris, after having come within sight of their goal, they were hounded and attacked from behind, further exacerbating a bad situation. By the following spring, only 50,000 of the original 500,000 French troops made it back to Paris.

Building a strategic plan is designing the conditions for the greatest probability of success in a contemplated conflict. Strategic planning must take into consideration the environment surrounding the conflict, which will ultimately have an influence on the outcome. Strategic planners of all kinds must not only take into consideration their own strengths, they must factor in their weaknesses as well. They must consider the strengths and the predictable behaviors of their opponent.

As high-level salespeople, you need to apply the same kind of thinking to your sales campaigns. You must become a strategic planner, calculating the conditions necessary for the greatest probability of success. As high-level salespeople, the stakes involved are higher, the cost of losing great. Not only are you risking a higher cost to execute a single sales campaign, but the opportunity cost is large, as well. In high-level selling, the average size of the opportunities you are competing for are much larger and much harder to replace when you lose. When you choose to compete, you cannot afford to lose.

In order to win more often, you need to become strategic thinkers and planners, building strategic plans that will create conditions for the greatest probability of success. You must carefully choose when you will and will not compete. You must factor in all aspects of the selling environment. You must consider the vitality of the customer, the goals and mission of the customer and the political environment of the customer organization. You must factor in your competitors, their strengths, weaknesses, and the strategies they are likely to use.

In order to build effective strategies, you need information. Strategic planning, done well, requires that you gather information, analyze that information to determine the most important factors of the selling environment and to assimilate those most important factors into a meaningful and effective strategy. From the strategy come the tactics, the physical acts, by which the customer and the competition will come to realize how you are prosecuting the sales campaign.

In business, there are several levels at which strategic planning should be applied. A coherent strategy will help organize whole companies into well-focused, successful businesses. Too often, in the absence of a meaningful strategy, companies languish, choosing multiple, disparate and disconnected directions, oftentimes in conflict with themselves. There are companies that strive to create a competitive internal culture that encourages this type of cross channel conflict and there is even some logic to support this kind of conflict. However, internal conflict, particularly when it is the result of an ambiguous strategy, is not a good thing.

A few years ago, the executive team of a particular division of a Fortune 100 company, found themselves in so many disparate businesses that it was nearly impossible for them to run their division. They were responsible for a business representing over $1 billion in revenue, but because they were running so many different kinds of businesses, there was no coherent strategy to support the whole organization. They were involved in information technology (their main business), maintenance contracts, buying and selling cleaning solutions and toilet paper, administrative support providing one of their customers with administrative assistants and several other lines of business. The reason this was a problem was that they were highly unprofitable in most of their business activities. They found themselves investing in so many different types of businesses that profitability seemed impossible. The lack of a coherent strategy caused them to disperse their efforts into businesses where they clearly did not belong. Ultimately, they were forced to divest all of their non-core business lines and focus on their main business in order to survive.

In the marketing organization, the use of strategy to launch products, organize product lines and coherently pursue market segments is vital. Marketing strategy, product strategy and pricing strategy can make the difference between success and failure.

Strategic planning can provide an individual, a sales team or even whole companies with the clarity required to move in concert toward common goals. Strategy and strategic planning, when skillfully and artfully constructed, can organize large groups of people into well-coordinated teams. Strategic planning can help them eliminate the activities that do not contribute to the common good. A strategic plan, in a relatively brief document, can organize massive quantities of activity into profitable operations.

The goal of Pursue Opportunity is to learn how to build strategic plans and how to protect those plans from your competition. You will learn how to determine when you should pursue a sales opportunity and when you should not. You will learn the components of a strategy and several planning formats so that you will understand how to build creative strategies that are meaningful and effective.

Strategy Defined

The concept of strategy originated 2,500 years ago in the book entitled The Art of War, written by the Chinese philosopher Sun Tzu. In that epoch of China's history, feudal lords controlled the population of their regions either harshly or benevolently with laws that were not codified or recorded. A feudal lord would hold or take more land by warring with his neighbors or by creating unrest in the local population. The Art of War has been the foundation for strategic thinking for thousands of years and has found applicability in endeavors other than waging war.

The root word for strategy comes from the Greek word strategos, which literally translated, means "the art of generals". While this may seem warlike to some, taken as a guideline, the "art of generals" implies a larger view of a conflict or a competition. Rather than focusing on the physical acts of competition, or tactics, strategy focuses on the big picture.

While we may be prepared to engage in sales, tactical engagement in the absence of a coherent strategy, often leads to waste and confusion. Building a strategy before you begin to execute tactics can be vital to your success.

Too often salespeople will eagerly go flailing into a sales situation based on their experience or on the coaching of their managers without first considering the approach or the strategy they should employ. In the case of a well-known customer, in a well-known market, and with well-known competition, this shoot first approach to selling might be sufficient to win. However, in competitive selling

Pursue Opportunity

situations that are critical to your success, the shoot first kind of selling often leads to disaster.

As a high-level salesperson, you are a consumer of information, information that comes from your research, questions and conversations with your prospects and customers. How you analyze that information and how you capitalize on that information is how you best apply your talents. Good information, early in the sales campaign is priceless; capitalizing on that information in a unique, professional, ethical and creative way will set you apart from your competitors.

In the context of selling, you should understand the word strategy to mean the approach, the pathway or the means by which you plan to achieve an objective or a goal. As you learn how to build a strategy and incorporate the strategy into your planning, you will come to appreciate the power and the clarity that comes from a well-defined strategy. Learning how to build effective strategies is not easy or simple. It can be frustrating and seem pointless, especially as you begin. However, it is the *art* of generals. Think of the development of a strategy as an art form.

If you decide to take guitar lessons in hopes of learning how to play music, you can familiarize yourself with the basics in a short time. It is the consistent practice of the art form, which will give you the ability to produce beautiful music. Practice, discipline and perseverance are the ingredients that help you to become a true strategic thinker, a real strategist.

Benefits of Strategic Planning

Questioning the value of strategic planning is common. Many times, its value will not be felt until late in the sales campaign. Salespeople and sales managers alike, who do not recognize the value of strategic thinking or strategic planning, will often jettison the strategy itself from their planning formats. This is, most often, a consequence of impatience and a lack of discipline.

Creating a good, well-reasoned strategy will yield many benefits. It will help you to become more effective, winning more business. It will help you to become more efficient. It will give you a clear, concise and meaningful message in your selling activities. It will help you better communicate with your customer and your colleagues, reducing the confusion that comes from the lack of a common language. It will provide you with a keener long-term focus, a vision of the future, and, the ability to measure and sense achievement.

Greater Effectiveness

By proactively pre-defining your strategy, you will be able to win more business. Because your strategy will take into account the customer's compelling business need and position that need with one of your unique strengths, the meaning and the power of your offering will be more evident to your prospects and customers. You will win more often because the customer's compelling business need is clearly positioned as requiring your offering.

Greater Efficiency

Strategic planning will enable you to allocate efficiently your limited resources, allowing you to pursue more opportunities with the same resources. Many salespeople have a tendency to misallocate their resources (especially their time) to tactics and activities that do not apply to their ultimate goal. In the presence of a clearly defined strategy, you will more easily be able to determine whether or not a given tactic or activity will help you advance toward your objective, eliminating unnecessary activity.

Clear Message

By pre-defining your strategy, you will come to a central, repeatable and meaningful message for your customer. By pre-defining your strategy, the customer will be able to recognize what you want them to know about your offering, and they should more easily recognize its significance.

As a salesperson, you are determined to convince prospects and customers as to the quality of your offering. You extol the virtues of the offering throughout a sales campaign. If you emphasize a particular strength in one meeting and a different strength in the next, you are sending multiple messages to the customer. In effect, these multiple messages confuse the customer more than they help the customer. Things only become more complicated when other people are involved in the same campaign. You are essentially confusing your customers with all these different messages and themes.

By creating a strategy, you are defining what your central theme for the sales campaign will be. Repeating that theme throughout the campaign will give you a consistent message. Your meaning will come through loud and clear.

Clear Communication

Strategic planning will give you and your colleagues a common language. Misunderstandings will become less common because you and your colleagues will speak the same language. You will find that the time it takes to come to a clear understanding with your colleagues will reduce drastically. You will all know the meaning of words like goal, objective or strategy. You will more easily be able to support each other, combining your collective strengths behind your strategy.

Clear Vision

Using the principles of strategic planning will give you the ability to create your own future, determining proactively where you want to be at some point in the future. The ability to develop effective strategies will help you meet your budgets and quotas with greater ease.

Think of a strategy as your compass, guiding your steps as you proceed through a competitive sales campaign. Particularly in the final phases of a selling effort when events become more chaotic and urgent, the sales strategy becomes your guidance system. It becomes the single message that clearly comes through to the customer as they make their decisions.

Pursue Opportunity

One of the most powerful indications that your strategy has been effective is when the customer repeats your theme and uses your logic to justify their buying decision. It is always satisfying to win business, but even more so when you designed and created the conditions for that success.

Building a Strategy Statement

Physically, the strategy statement must answer two key questions in a single statement or sentence, "Why?" and, "What?" "Why should the customer do business with me/us?" and, "What am I counting on to succeed?"

The basic construction of a strategy is simple; answer those two questions and put the answers into a single, rational, memorable sentence. However, the quality of your thinking and analysis will determine whether your strategy will be effective.

Why Should the Customer Do Business with Me/Us?

The answer to this first question is all about the customer. It is the customer's compelling business issue that is (or should be) driving them to make a buying decision. The customer's compelling business factor drives their buying process.

The answer to this question has nothing to do with you or your company. It has nothing to do with any other factor from your side of the sales situation. The compelling business factor is in the customer's buying environment, value chain, market situation or business plan. What is the compelling factor that is forcing them to take this decision now? What business need is most critically harming or hindering the customer?

What Am I Counting on to Succeed?

What potential differentiator can you position that will address the first question, "why?" The answer to this second question is about you, but only about a strength that rationally relates to the customer's compelling factor. It is your professional analysis of their situation (the Why?) and your creative solution or strength (the What?) combined into a single sentence that will give your strategy meaning and strength.

Building a Strategy Statement

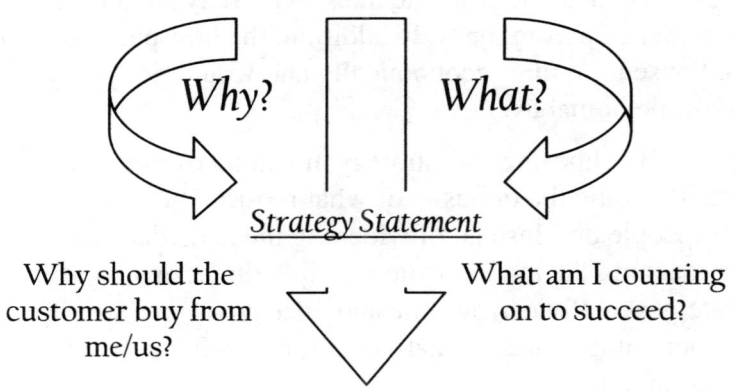

"Position the home as a collector's item with a rising Aurora native." This might be a good example of a strategy statement. It might be ideal for a homeowner selling an older home in Aurora, Illinois. If we take the statement apart and look at its components, we begin to see how the two key questions, "Why?" and "What?" are answered.

The strategy statement implies several things. First, the home is not new. It is a "collector's item", and should be valued for the older attributes of the house. This answers the question, "What am I counting on to succeed?" The strategy selects a characteristic of the home as a differentiator. There are probably many other differentiators, but the one differentiator the homeowner selected is "collector's item". The homeowner selected the differentiator in the context of the ideal buyer, according to the analysis of the selling situation.

Next, the ideal buyer for the house would be a "native" Auroran, someone who would fully appreciate the history of the house and the city. This answers, in two parts in this instance, the strategic question, "Why should the customer buy from me?" In addition, the best purchaser for the house is "rising" economically and would not likely be a first-time homebuyer.

By choosing this strategy, the homeowner is actually doing the opposite of what most real estate salespeople do. Instead of widening the audience and approaching the market from multiple directions, this strategy actually narrows the audience down to a specific segment of the market - native Aurorans who are rising economically.

Is this a wise decision? Should the audience be narrowed to a sub-set of the total buying universe? Conventional wisdom dictates that the house should sell to the first person that wants to buy it. Conventional wisdom suggests that the homeowner would not want to limit the market.

Pursue Opportunity

In this case, as in many cases, conventional wisdom would be wrong. You want to limit the market to those people that would have the highest appreciation for the house. By doing so, you get a meaningful, focused message to the ideal audience. By doing so, you eliminate the need to try to be all things to all people.

What would happen if a younger buyer from out of town wanted to buy the house? Would we refuse to sell the house to them? Probably not, but this buyer would not have the same level of appreciation for an older house. They would not appreciate the historical nature of the house. They would probably not be willing to pay the same price for the house as a person who does appreciate the historical attributes. They would bid less and perhaps ask for certain concessions that the ideal buyer would not ask for.

The strategy also establishes a central theme for the sales campaign. "Collectors Item for Sale" may sound corny to you, but it is more motivating than "House for Sale". You could use this theme in your tactics. When you advertise the house in the newspaper, the theme becomes the large print for the ad, Collectors Item for Sale. Instead of describing the features of the house, you could write a short story entitled Collector's Item for Sale, detailing the historical significance of the house. Instead of putting up a traditional House for Sale sign, you could put up a large sign in the front yard saying, Collector's Item for Sale.

This strategy also helps to optimize resources. Based on the analysis that created the strategy, the ideal buyer is an Aurora native. This approach would eliminate the need to advertise outside the immediate Aurora area, using the ad budget locally.

In high-level, B2B selling, the sales situation is different and perhaps more complex than in this example. In our example, we were selling a single home to a group of customers with certain characteristics. However, the strategy you build for B2B selling will answer the same two strategic questions as in our example. In the B2B space, you are focusing on a specific customer rather than on a group of potential buyers. In the B2B space, you have a better sense of who your competitors are or could be. The construction of the strategy would be the same as in our example. You would answer, in a single statement, the two strategic questions. Why should the customer buy from me/us? What am I counting on to succeed?

Types of Strategies

> "When your forces are stronger than your enemy's, surround him, attack him and divide him. When your forces are less than your enemy's, fight with clever tactics, hold your ground and evade him. In addition, there must be exceptional leadership to attain the goals of the conflict; otherwise there will be the danger of suffering an agonizing defeat."
>
> <u>The Art of War</u> by Sun Tzu

As you develop your own sales strategies for specific sales campaigns, you will begin to notice that strategies fall into six primary categories. Depending on the selling environment, the customer and the competition, you will create strategies that fall into one of the following categories.

Preemption Strategy

In the case of overwhelming superiority, the Preemption strategy effectively says, you will take your offering to the customer before your competitor has a chance to fully prepare and engage in the competition. Surprise, speed and overwhelming superiority will allow you to win. In military terms, it is the concentration of overwhelming strength and the rapid execution of the plan.

Strike before the enemy is fully aware that a competition is under way.

You use the Preemption strategy when you have several key factors in place. You have an existing presence with the customer, and they are happy with the relationship. You have a presence and the support of the senior executives in the account. This senior executive support is present where you have regular contact with them, as well as others outside your normal areas of operation. Your association with the customer includes the political support of the most powerful people in the account. In addition, your offering is complete and satisfactory compared to the proposed buying criteria of the customer.

Head-to-Head Strategy

This strategy implies straightforward, Head-to-Head competition. It is a frontal assault in a sales campaign pitting you and your strengths directly at the stated buying criteria of the customer. In the customer's estimation, you are superior. You are pitting one or more of your traditional strengths of product, price, relationships or your company's image and reputation against your competitor's lesser strengths.

The requirements for choosing the Head-to-Head strategy are first a good reputation or installed base with the customer. It is nearly impossible to execute this strategy if your history with the customer is questionable. Next, there needs to be a compelling business factor already present with the customer to proceed with the purchase. It is possible to create this compelling business reason, but that would best be done with a different strategy. Finally, the buying criteria as defined by the customer and your offering must be more compatible than your competitor's. It is not enough to say that your offering is superior; the customer must be saying that your offering is superior.

The Head-to-Head strategy is the modus operandi for the salesperson that operates in a traditional fashion. Where little or no thought is given to strategy, the default strategy is a Head-to-Head strategy. As the salesperson fails in the effort to advance, he will retrench and attempt a different approach. To show the customer and your competitors a change in your sales strategy is a clear act of desperation.

Flanking Strategy

The Flanking strategy is a non-traditional strategy that implies that your offering is not enough, in itself, to win the business. It may be that your price is not as low as the competition's or that you have a non-existent or weak history with the customer. In the Flanking strategy, we will set out to change the rules of the engagement, utilizing a unique and unconventional approach.

The Flanking strategy is creative and challenging because it requires considerably more thought to find one unique approach that will create the conditions for winning the business. The Flanking strategy is creative and non-traditional, approaching the sales campaign from a different direction with a different kind of message.

Most often, to be effective with a Flanking strategy, the senior management or the politically powerful people must become involved in making the buying decision. They are not usually part of the formal decision process, but rather part of the informal decision process. Creative tactics employed in the execution of a Flanking strategy must compel these people to become involved. These people must be given a compelling alternate to their existing buying criteria where your competitor is favored.

Another critical aspect of the Flanking strategy is timing. Thinking forward to the point at which you will be attempting to change the rules, what will be the response of the competition when they realize they are no longer favored and must adjust to the new version of the buying criteria? If you are executing a Flanking strategy, you should try to do so at a point in time when the competition has no possibility of recovering.

Partition Strategy

The Partition strategy implies that you cannot win the whole order, or deliver the entire application for the customer's needs so you will compete for only part of the business. Rather than giving up altogether or competing for the entire project, which you would surely lose, competing for only a portion of the business can be an option. It is a viable option against an entrenched competitor whose relationship with the customer is solid. It is the classic beachhead strategy, where your goal might be to use this win to expand your presence with the account.

If integration between your offering and the incumbent is an issue, you must be able to coexist peacefully. Your offering cannot represent a radical change. It must appear as effortless to the customer as though they bought from their main supplier.

Pursue Opportunity

For example, if integration of technologies is required to get your system and the incumbent's system to work together, do not expect the customer to pick up the cost. If platform migration is an issue, do not expect the customer to pay. Do not expect the customer to pay for any of the additional expenses that might be required to get the two offerings to function as one. In those types of situations, you must pick up the incremental costs, since the customer would not have similar costs were they to buy from their current supplier.

If multiple maintenance systems are required, there is the possibility that the customer may have no one to hold accountable when problems arise, each supplier blaming the other.

The typical message of a Partition strategy revolves around the customer's need for diversification of providers: "Don't put all your eggs in one basket." The typical response from a competitor facing a Partition strategy is the risk associated with multiple suppliers since each will likely blame the other in the event of a problem. Accountability is an issue, which needs to be proactively dealt with when using a Partition strategy.

Consortium Strategy

The development of alliances in business today is becoming more common. In large or complex sales campaigns, the proactive construction of a consortium can be a powerful persuader to customers. It can give you credibility and increase the size and scope of your offerings. The theme that arises from a Consortium strategy will typically sound similar to Partition strategies, "Don't put all your eggs in one basket." However, instead of sharing the basket with your competitor, you are sharing the basket with your allied companies, your consortium.

Some years ago EDS was competing for a $4.2 billion outsource contract against CSC, their main competitor. J.P. Morgan was the customer and had been a happy EDS customer for several years. They were so happy, in fact, that their CIO had been featured in one of EDS' annual reports, extolling the virtues of their relationship with EDS.

The strategy of EDS was a Head-to-Head strategy, directly leveraging their relationships with J.P. Morgan and their size. They were trying to convince them that they were the only company capable of handling an outsourcing contract of that size. Under the circumstances, EDS was confident that they would prevail and win the business, which to that point would have been the largest outsourcing contract ever placed.

CSC has a rich history in computer technology and service provision, having come from the military and government sectors where they had played major roles with various prestigious implementations over many years. Their primary weakness in this campaign, however, was one of EDS's key points: CSC was not big enough to handle a contract of this size. At that time, CSC was only about $4 billion a year in revenue versus EDS' $13 billion, so it was easy to convince J.P. Morgan that CSC could not handle the business.

CSC effectively used a Consortium strategy by going out and putting together a group of other companies to deliver the proposed services. They developed alliances with Accenture, AT&T and Nynex (a consortium) to overcome their perceived weakness due to a lack of size. In fact, a main part of their message to J.P. Morgan was that no single company, even EDS, was large enough to handle the size of the service contract that was being contemplated. They were able to co-opt EDS' message by essentially agreeing with it and then doing something about it. They developed a consortium.

Contain Strategy

The objective of the Contain strategy is not the same as in the other strategies. In the other strategies, the objective is your product, price and time. In the Contain strategy, the objective is to prevent the customer from making a decision until you are ready to compete or you are able to deliver.

Key in the execution of the Contain strategy is getting to the higher-level audience with a compelling business reason to halt their buying process. It is not effective at the lower, operational levels of a company. In fact, if the lower audience finds out that you are attempting to delay their purchase, they might not take it well.

The higher-level audience is the audience with the interest in your business case to stall the purchase. The higher-level audience, the audience with the power, has the ability to stop the buying process. You must get to the right audience and you must give them the business case for the delay.

The Contain strategy is a viable option for any size competitor, but it is easiest for the large, highly credible competitor. The Contain strategy has proven effective for many companies over the years, like IBM, Microsoft and even Infiniti automobiles.

In the early years of the computer revolution, companies were unsure about their requirements or the usefulness of computing platforms. They relied heavily on IBM initially, but eventually on other big name computer companies. IBM was famous for capitalizing on the insecurities of the technology-buying corporation. Their advertising theme for several years was, "Nobody ever got fired for buying IBM." It was very effective in preying on the technological insecurity of companies. As such, IBM was able to not only charge more for their technology, but they were able to get customers to delay needed purchases sometimes for years.

There was a well-known waiting list of purchasers for IBM's products, some waiting for deliveries as far out as two or more years. Articles in the Wall Street Journal used to report that customers would buy positions in the IBM queue for tens of thousands of dollars just to move up their delivery by a few months. This is an example of a Contain strategy.

When Microsoft was developing their first major operating system improvement, moving toward the pull-down menu, point-and-click world, their release date for Windows 95 was October of 1994. In the software business, the cooperation of software development companies and manufacturers is vital to a successful launch. In addition, IBM was trying to establish their operating system, the OS2.

When it became apparent that Windows 95 would not be ready to launch on schedule, rather than simply let the world go on without them, Microsoft launched a Contain strategy. They advertised a non-existent product. They assembled the largest test group for a beta version ever assembled. They went out all over the world doing public demonstrations of the software. They gave away free demo disks in hotels, airports and stores. They were actively selling a product that could not be delivered.

In October of 1995, they were finally able to release the product. After a full year of selling and marketing the platform, effectively stalling software developers, computer manufacturers and the computer buying public all year long, they finally brought the product to market with even more fanfare. The demand that they had been successful in developing throughout the year finally culminated with excited buyers lining up in the middle of the night at stores all over the world.

When Lexus introduced their luxury car to North America, Infiniti was not ready to bring their car to market. Instead of simply sitting there and waiting for the launch date of their car, they advertised. While the Lexus commercials were able to show their cars and invite buyers into the showroom to buy a car, Infiniti's ads showed pictures of babbling brooks or similar nature scenes, but no cars at all. They did not have a car to show in the commercials, so, instead of waiting, they advertised anyway. Their message to the consumers of luxury automobiles was, "Wait! Do not buy that Lexus until you have seen the Infiniti. We'll make it worth your while."

These are all examples of Contain strategies where companies were unable to deliver a product, and yet unwilling to concede customers to their competition. The software industry refers to this kind of sales campaign as "vaporware" - no product, a lot of hype and a market waiting to buy. It is, of course, critical that you actually deliver value at the end of the wait. Some companies have created too much hype and not enough products, leaving their credibility damaged and sometimes even putting the company out of business.

Do you remember a company called Osborn Computer? Back in the early 1980's, they were the first company to come to market with a portable computer, if forty pounds is portable. The Osborn One was the first computer built to travel from the office to the home. The company was highly successful, reaching $30 million in revenue within their first six months of doing business, a record at the time. They were adored by Wall Street and the investing public. They were one of the earliest high-tech, high-flier stocks.

When Compaq brought their version of the portable computer to market, they introduced a machine that was lighter and somewhat more powerful than the Osborn One. They immediately gained market share and the public's attention. The response from Osborn was to tell the world that if they liked the Osborn One, "just wait until you see the Osborn Two." Their intention was to stall the sales of the Compaq machine and, for a time, it seemed that the Contain strategy was going to work.

In fact, it worked very well. So well, that the market stalled on the Osborn One, killing their source of funds for the completion of the Osborn Two and leaving them with warehouses full of Osborn One's. They scrambled to Wall Street for more investors to finish the project, but were never able to complete the Osborn Two.

They had run their Contain strategy so well that they contained themselves out of business.

It is possible to use the Contain strategy in a sales campaign. It is also possible to do it so well that you convince the customer that they really do not need the contemplated purchase. They did well enough for this long without it, they can do with out it permanently. Be careful with the Contain strategy; you may contain yourself out of an order.

Selecting the Right Strategy

The type of strategy that you select for any given sales campaign is dependent on your position with the customer and with your competition. The type of strategy will also depend on the resources available to you to execute the campaign. Are you strong or weak? Is your reputation with the customer good or bad? Is your offering what they are looking for, or do they clearly prefer your competitor?

There are conditions in each sales campaign that will influence the type of strategy you choose. These conditions will lead you to use either the Preemption, Head-to-Head, Flanking, Partition, Consortium or Contain strategy as the most appropriate type of strategy.

Competitive Scenarios

Based on your company, your industry and your offerings, you will find yourself in competitive situations that will likely fall into one of several categories. The category can provide you with some insight as to which type of strategy would work best in your strategic plan.

Battle of Equals

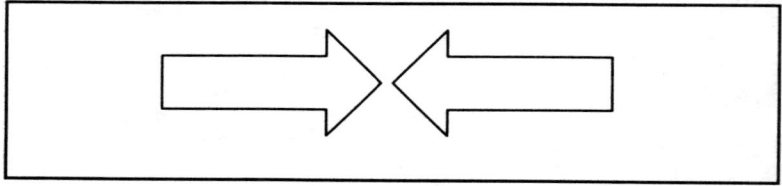

Pursue Opportunity

In this selling situation, you and your competitor are roughly equal and undifferentiated from the customer's perspective. While you may feel that your offering is superior for a variety of reasons, the customer does not agree. It is possible that the customer has done business with both you and your competitor in the past. Neither you nor your competition has a large enough presence with the customer to be considered entrenched.

Analysis

In this type of situation, you do not have superior force and, therefore, the Head-to-Head strategy would not be a good choice. If you feel you could do the entire application of the contemplated purchase, then that would eliminate the Partition and the Consortium strategies. The use of the Contain strategy would not be appropriate if you are in a position to deliver the offering and compete in the campaign. In addition, if a compelling business issue is present and it is a high priority for the customer, the business basis you would have to offer the customer to stop their buying process would have to be even more compelling.

A Flanking strategy would work best in this situation. If there is a compelling business issue that is a priority for the customer, then your strategy should be concentrated on connecting their compelling business issue with some non-traditional aspect of your offering. Connecting those two things can be an attractive combination for the customer. It would also be difficult for your competition to replicate.

David vs. Goliath

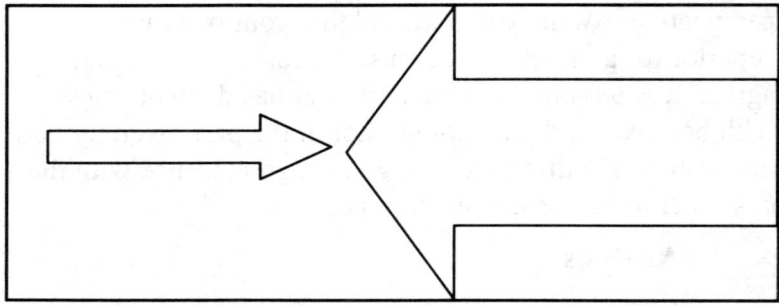

In this selling situation, you are David in the classic fight. You have no presence with the customer and your competitor is well known. There are personal relationships between your competitor and individuals at all levels of the customer organization. The customer is familiar and comfortable in the utilization of your competitor's offering.

Analysis

The Head-to-Head strategy is not appropriate because you do not have superior force. The Contain strategy would not be appropriate, either, since the customer would likely proceed with their well-known supplier.

Perhaps the best choice would be the Partition strategy. In this strategy, you would focus on a subset of the customer's total purchase that involves a particular strength for you or your company. Your strategy would use a traditional strength as its core message, capitalizing on product, price or reputation. The customer does not know if they are doing as well as they could or should because they have limited their sources to the incumbent supplier. The Partition strategy, focusing on only a portion of the total application, would not involve the same level of risk for the customer as adopting a new supplier for their entire application.

Another option would be the Consortium strategy, where you would purposefully put together an alliance of partner companies to displace the incumbent supplier. It would be necessary for the alliance to appear seamless to the customer with a single point of accountability. It would need to represent a more compelling offering than the incumbent as well, to avoid ending up in a battle of equals. You may be able to present a way for the customer, on a continuing basis, to be assured of the latest and best the consortium has to offer since the customer would be exposed to new developments from multiple sources.

The last strategy choice would be the Flanking strategy. Your strategy would have to focus on the potential risks in limiting the customer's options to the status quo. In other words, the customer is assuming an unknown risk by doing business with only one supplier. Your Flanking strategy would be a negative approach, pointing out areas of potential weakness in the customer's value chain. You will not succeed with the lower, operational audience because they are usually change resistant. The correct audience would be the higher-level managers and the executives. They would not be threatened personally by the negative tones of your campaign and would be able to respond to the risks that you are uncovering.

Goliath vs. David

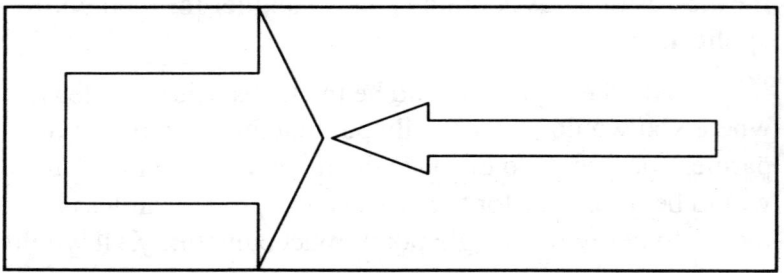

Here, you are the dominant player in the account with a long standing and successful relationship. You have many friends inside the account and are intimately familiar with the business issues facing the customer. You are aware of other companies who are trying to enter into your space, but you have been successful at repelling the attacks.

Analysis

It would be ideal to use the Preemption strategy, preventing the release of new selling opportunities to your competition. You would capitalize on your intimate working relationship with the customer to win the business before the rest of your industry is aware of the opportunity. Winning without having to compete is inexpensive.

However, in competitive situations where you are dominant, the best strategy would be the Head-to-Head strategy. You want to compete at the highest appropriate levels in the account and limit the availability of the customer to your competitor by engaging with the customer in their buying process. Your strategy would be based on your existing relationships with the customer and emphasize the customer's wisdom in having selected you in the past.

Pursue Opportunity

The Flanking, Partition and Consortium strategies would not be good choices in this type of situation. The Contain strategy would be necessary if a competitor has been able to generate interest in a new technology that you do not offer. In this case, you can contain the buying process by showing that your coming offering will include or perhaps exceed the competition's. You will have to provide a solid business basis for supporting the delay in the buying process.

Commodity Brokers

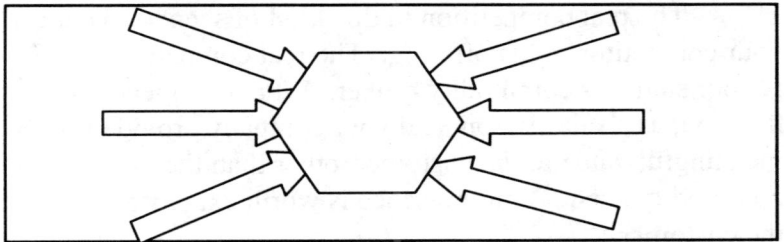

You and your company are well known. The customer may even consider you critical to their success. Your offering does not represent anything new, and the customer is completely familiar with the usage of your offering. The primary concerns expressed by the customer regarding your offering are price and delivery. The quality of your offering is assumed by the customer to be the industry's standard level of quality and equal to your competitor's quality. Your primary concern from a competitive perspective is that one of your competitors will drop their price to a level that is untenable for you.

Analysis

This is a very common and very difficult position. A Head-to-Head strategy will only lead you to deeper discounts and expensive sales campaigns. The Partition strategy would only support your commoditized competitor, sacrificing some percentage of your business with no gain to you or the customer. The Contain strategy would be useless as well. In order for the Contain strategy to work, you have to provide a solid business basis supporting the delay. Since the competition's product is the same as yours, it would be difficult to come up with the business basis.

The real competition in this kind of scenario is not your competitor or his offering. The real competition here is your status as commodity broker. What this means is that you, as a salesperson, and your company provide no meaningful value to the customer, other than the commodity itself. Your presence is worth exactly zero with the customer.

In order for you to break out of this death-spiral situation, you must actively engage with the customer in non-traditional ways that they would not expect from you or your company. You cannot do this with the lower level audience since they already recognize you as a supplier of undifferentiated commodities. You must go to a different audience. When you go to these other audiences, you cannot talk about yourself or your product. Doing so will only send you back to the original audience with the inevitable castigation that goes with having been caught outside of your acceptable boundaries. Instead, use the CVO approach, focusing on the creation of value from the customer's perspective.

Pursue Opportunity

One type of strategy suitable in this kind of scenario is the Flanking strategy, and then only if you are willing to risk your current position with the customer. The Flanking strategy should be focused on the creation of a larger, customer-oriented value proposition that would have to be broader than your traditional business. You would do this at higher levels in the organization with a new level of consultative behavior, helping them explore new ways of running their business. Your focus is the value chain, their business processes and creating new and unique ways of solving broader problems.

Evangelists

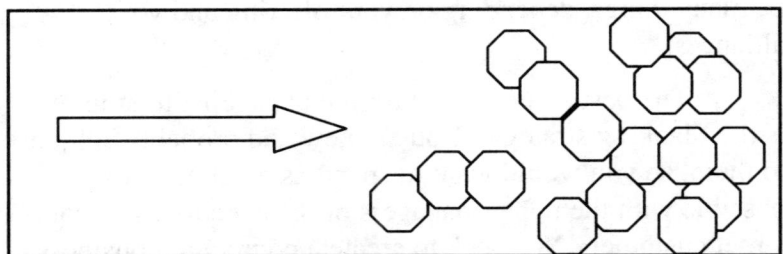

Your job as an evangelist is to open up new markets for your company. Your offering may be well known in other types of markets, but your presence in this market is new. Both you and your company may have great credibility in your original markets. You are attempting to win new converts in these new markets.

Analysis

This is a difficult problem because you are trying to compel customers to begin a new and entirely different buying process. You are asking the customer to create new budget category to buy your offering. The budget might come from other categories or you might need to compel them to create new budget entirely. In either case, you are the outsider, the unknown.

The Head-to-Head strategy would not be useful in this situation since there is no experience either from the customer or from your company in the proposed areas of business. There is no compelling business issue driving the customer's buying process.

The Partition and the Consortium strategies may have merit, depending on your specific offering. In the Partition strategy, your message would be "proof of concept". In the Consortium strategy, your message could be many things, depending on your offering and your alliances.

The best strategy type for the evangelist to employ is the Flanking strategy. You are new and probably unique to them, so you would want to spend as much time as possible with the upper managers or the executives of your target customer. You seek to create a compelling business issue that will help the customer initiate their buying process. Using the CVO approach, you would spend much of your time helping them justify the investment in your offering using ROI, Payback Period or some other financial model.

Pursue Opportunity

Disruptors

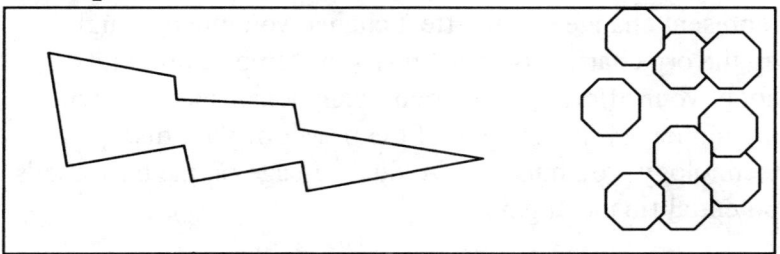

You have a disruptive technology that is in its early market acceptance phase. Your offering is vastly superior in technological terms and is dramatically cheaper than the former alternatives. You are attacking a well-known market that has a well-known solution with an offering that is dramatically better due to a technological breakthrough. You expect to become a "category killer" but are still in the early adoption phases.

Analysis

Because of your obvious product superiority, you will be tempted to use the Head-to-Head strategy most often. You will want to spend your time with the lower level, technical types who would appreciate your disruptive technology. You would want to receive the feedback that invariably comes from showing something to customers that is truly disruptive technology. You would also be wrong.

The best strategy choice for this situation is a Flanking strategy. Even though your offering is clearly superior, the power to change existing business processes and current relationships does not lie in the lower levels. The power to change lies with the senior managers up to the executives. Even though your product is superior, you represent change and to affect change you must go higher up the org chart. You must resist the temptation to talk about your offering or your company when speaking with the higher levels. In spite of the power of your disruptive technology, you must focus your message on the customer's potential financial gain.

The Best Strategy

There is no single answer for any given sales situation that is correct and all others incorrect. Selecting the right strategy is not that simple. As you build your strategic plan, first decide which type of strategy would be best and then build the strategy statement. If you are not happy with the strategy at that point, return to the profile and look for alternatives.

When you first begin to use strategic planning, creating the best strategy can be difficult. The planning session is an exercise of poring over the information, searching for that single approach that will differentiate you from your competitors. This will take more time as you begin, but with practice, you will gain proficiency. This will reduce the time of the planning session dramatically.

How do you know if you have created the right strategy? At what point should you stop thinking about your strategic options and select a single strategy?

The creation of the right strategy is usually emotional. You will feel better about one strategy as compared to other strategic options. If you have gathered enough good information and analyzed it well, the strategy you select will be effective.

Pursue Opportunity 93

Even if you are not wildly enthusiastic about the strategy you create, it is better than no strategy at all. In strategic planning, it is better to be wrong than confused. Being right is the best thing, of course. However, absent that outcome, the wrong strategy will at least serve to put you and your sales campaign in motion in a single direction. If you later find that it is not an effective strategy, you can and should change strategy. This is not ideal, but at least your sales campaign is already in motion. If you are confused, your sales campaign may be in motion, but your mixed-messages and tactical confusion will be scattered throughout the customer organization and your own, creating chaos.

In 1992, when Bill Clinton first ran for president, he was only one of six candidates for the Democratic Party. He was not the favored candidate when he began his campaign, but he was strategic. He had a concentrated, central theme that was adopted very early in his quest. His theme was "Change", 12 years of Ronald Reagan and George H. Bush was enough. The country needs "change".

He used his "change" theme day in and day out. He would support the theme with evidence of a stagnating economy or a broken health care system. When featured on the news, he used the central theme repeatedly. Even in the face of George H. Bush's historically high approval ratings during the Gulf War, Bill Clinton stayed on message: "Change; 12 years of Republicans is enough."

At the beginning of the campaign, there seemed to be little relevance to his strategy. The other democratic hopefuls all seemed to be saying many different things with no coherent strategy. As is often the case in politics in the United States, the candidates spent some of their airtime attacking each other. Through it all, however, Bill Clinton had the discipline to stay with his central theme.

Finally, only months before the election, his message seemed to be gaining credibility and significance. As evidence of the slowing US economy began to appear the "Change" strategy started working. The theme started catching on. It was his good fortune that the economy was slowing, enhancing the significance of his message. It also helped that President Bush was denying that the economy was actually slowing. It also helped that in spite of having said, "Read my lips", Bush signed legislation to raise taxes. In the context of these events, Clinton's central theme gained real credibility.

Strategic planning, selecting the right strategy and sticking to it, requires discipline and courage. Before you change your strategy, make sure your new strategy is better than your current strategy. Changing strategies just before your original strategy gains credibility would be a disaster.

The Corporate Agenda

The strategic planner is one who is capable of finding clarity in complexity, calm in chaos, direction and purpose when others are wandering aimlessly. The strategic thinker is able to better understand the environment around them and with that understanding, take meaningful action toward their goals and objectives.

This clarity in chaos comes from an ability to better articulate the environment around them in such a way that direction and purpose become obvious. This clarity is impossible to achieve in the absence of good information. Your experience in similar situations may provide you with the guidance system that a strategy would otherwise provide. However, absent those experiences, in a volatile market environment, the outcome you seek would be mostly a matter of luck.

The point to strategic planning is to position yourself and your offering in the best possible light in relation to your customer and in relation to your competitor. Strategic planning is creating the conditions necessary for the greatest possibility of success. The ultimate win is designed and pre-planned. The ultimate win comes from your ability to control the outcome of a sales campaign because of the strategy that you created.

Strategic Planning Terminology

There are many ways of saying the same thing relating to the formats for strategic planning. Some of the common terms that companies use are Initiatives, Vision

Statements, Objectives and Goals. What we will be putting into place here is a hierarchy of the terms that are applicable to many different forms of strategic planning. These terms are useful in clarifying chaos and understanding complex situations. By understanding these terms, you will be able to understand more clearly complex selling situations.

Corporate Mission

A mission statement is an articulated statement that spells out the purpose of existence. It explains why an organization exists. The mission statement hangs in the lobby of the corporation for the entire world to see.

The mission statement, well articulated, is a statement that gives the organization a sense of purpose and meaning, la raison d'être. A well articulated mission statement should answer the questions, "Who are we?" and "Why do we exist?" A mission statement becomes the guiding light for the company. The presence of a meaningful mission statement enables whole companies to make good, decisions independent of management input. A mission statement embodies the standing orders that other activities are to support, and if the activities do not support the mission, then the activity must be eliminated. Companies are able to make investment decisions based on their mission statement.

The absence of a well-articulated mission statement leads to several problems: lack of identity, low employee morale and customer confusion. A poorly articulated mission statement leads to corporate schizophrenia, a company with multiple personalities. A mission statement that is not believable leads to apathy and change-resistance.

Corporate Goals

Goals are directional in nature, giving whole companies the sense of direction that supports their company's mission. It is not enough, of course, to define in simple terms the mission statement. Companies must also give everyone, including their customers, some sense of the direction they are heading. Other terms that generally mean the same thing as goal are Vision Statements or Corporate Initiatives. These terms have a place in strategic planning, but their meaning is the same as goal.

Goals, well articulated, should provide the direction the team should be heading in, the cardinal points of movement. A poorly articulated goal may do more damage than good. If the goal is too vague, it becomes subject to interpretation leaving the directional nature of the goal to the subjective conclusion of the individual. This causes companies to start initiatives but seldom complete them. Conversely, if the goal is too specific, the danger might be that some good opportunities are not pursued.

Corporate Objectives

An objective, properly articulated, should clearly define the steps that are essential for moving in the direction of your goal. An objective is much more concrete than a goal. An objective is distinguished by your ability to determine when you are finished. There is a well-defined end to an objective. An objective should always be specific, measurable and time bound; "We need 10 red hula hoops by 3 o'clock this afternoon."

An acronym that applies to a well-articulated objective is the "S.M.A.R.T." principle: Specific, Measurable, Achievable, Realistic and Time Bound.

Tactics

A tactic is a physical act. The tactic must advance toward your objective. It must support your strategy. If the tactic does not do these two things, then do not use it. If you were to use an unrelated tactic, you would be wasting your resources, especially your irreplaceable time resource. If you execute an unrelated tactic, you run the risk of confusing your customer.

Tactics are the physical acts that give motion to your campaign. In selling situations, tactics can be presentations, phone calls, research and other activities that relate to your sales campaign. Tactics become the physical manifestation of what your strategy, what your central theme for the sales campaign will be. It is not appropriate to convey your strategy to a customer. The customer, as well as your competitors, will become aware of your strategy through your tactics.

The combination of mission, goals, objectives and tactics into one well-reasoned plan is a Corporate Agenda. It will serve you well to be able to apply it to your company, your customer's company and your sales campaigns and even to your personal life. Understanding the framework of the Corporate Agenda enables you to find clarity in complexity. It allows you to quickly grasp and manage complexity.

The Corporate Agenda

The Application of Strategy to a Corporate Agenda

The corporate agenda is the primary tool available to you to build a strategic plan. Why isn't the strategy statement a part of the corporate agenda?

The answer is that there is a fundamental distinction between "Who?" we are (mission statement), "Where?" we are going (goal), what "Steps?" we must take (objective) and what must we "Do?" (tactics). The strategy is "How?" or "What approach?" you use to accomplish a mission, goal, objective or tactic. Each component of the corporate agenda is a destination, a hoped-for future state or a specific step or action.

When the success of a mission, goal, objective or tactic is in doubt because of the complexity of the situation, then a strategy is required. For example, if your objective were to go to the grocery store for a few items, you would not need a strategy. The situation is not so complex that your success is in doubt. A strategy is not necessary because you have been to the store many times and know exactly where you are going. However, if you were hosting a dinner for 30 people, you might want to give some thought to a strategy. Dealing with the complexity of the objective, hosting a dinner for 30 people on Saturday night, could be easier if you work out a strategy.

Sales Planning Formats

There are several different strategic planning formats. The format you choose will depend on the level of complexity of the sales situation. If it is a complex selling situation, involving multiple sales objectives, then the format for your strategic plan could include all of the components of the Corporate Agenda. If your selling situation is not complex, you might use only a part of the Corporate Agenda. The strategic planning format that you select should fit the challenge of the selling situation.

Objective, Strategy, Tactics

The "O.S.T." format of strategic planning is suitable for less complex selling situations, particularly when you need to focus on one critical sales objective. The O.S.T. format will force you and your organization to focus directly on one specific sales objective.

Objective

Your sales objective is a single sentence that incorporates your offering, price and time frame. It is the definition in the clearest terms possible of what you want to accomplish. In a sales campaign, your objective would usually be to win an order for business. This would include the product or service (in very specific terms) of what you'd like to sell, the price or financial terms you believe you can get for the offering and finally the time frame in which you realistically believe you can achieve the objective. If your customer is large and complex, other descriptions inside the objective are acceptable, but only if they clarify what you want to achieve.

Strategy

The strategy statement is the single unifying, directional statement. It is the statement of how you will achieve your sales objective. The strategy is a single sentence that answers the two central questions, "Why should the customer do business with me/us?" and, "What am I counting on to succeed?" It should be memorable and thematic in nature so that you will not have to refer back to your written statement. A well-articulated strategy can frequently be reduced down to a slogan, a short catch phrase that characterizes the whole strategy. The strategy should be shared with your sales organization so that they can directly support your thrust in the selling situation.

A well-reasoned and well-articulated strategy should only be fashioned after sufficient profile and analysis have been performed. If you attempt to build a strategy statement without sufficient information and analysis, either your strategy will be flawed causing you to recreate the strategy later or the strategy will be ineffective.

Tactics

These are the physical acts that will advance your strategy. They must support your strategy in a direct way, clearly advancing your strategic theme with the customer. This means that at the beginning of your presentations, the beginning of your meetings, the beginning of your phone conversations with the customer, your theme is the message. This means that every tactic you consider must support, in a direct fashion, your strategy. If the tactic does not support your strategy, then do not use the tactic.

G.O.S.T. Format

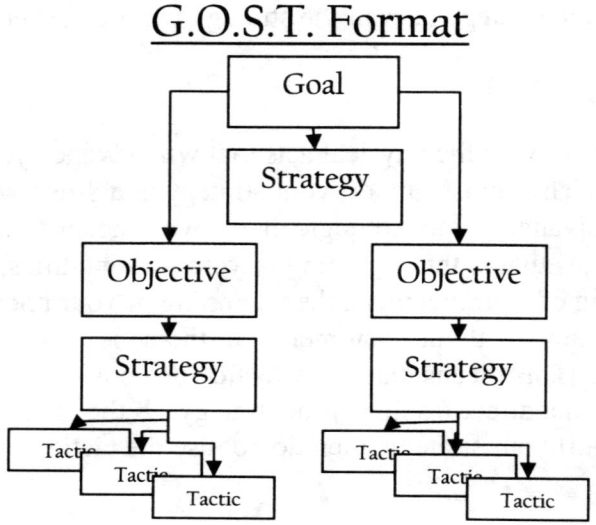

Goal, Objective, Strategy, Tactics

The G.O.S.T. planning format is best in complex selling situations. This format would be suitable for an important national account with a team of dedicated people from your company. It would work well in situations where you are responsible for a large geographic territory involving many different customers.

Goal

The G.O.S.T. format begins with a goal describing some future position. It may be a revenue goal for a sales team dedicated to a national account. It may be a revenue target for a territory. Other goals might be to achieve "preferred vendor status" with a particular customer or become the "number one provider" in a geographic region.

Pursue Opportunity

Objectives

Each goal would have several objectives, steps that would move you toward your goal. These objectives, as before, would be more specific and time bound. Sales objectives include the product or the service you would like to sell, the price you would like to sell it for and the time frame in which you would like to sell it. In complex situations of national or global accounts, you would also need to identify the customer division that relates to the objective. For example, "Obtain a signed contract for 2 XBR 90's (product) for $1.5 million each (price) by October 31 of this year (time) with the Dallas, Texas manufacturing facility."

Strategy

You would develop a strategy for each of the objectives whether the objective is a sales objective or some other type of objective. The only time that a strategy would not be necessary for an objective is when the objective itself is simple, clear, familiar and eminently doable. Otherwise, build a strategy for each of your plan's objectives.

Tactics

For each of your objectives and supporting the strategies, you will have a group of tactics that give motion to the plan. Without tactics, strategic planning, no matter how elegant and well designed, will never succeed.

Mission, Goals, Objective, Tactics

When challenged with the most complex selling situations, start your planning at the top of the Corporate Agenda. The "M.G.O.T." plan accommodates large selling environments, many people, several goals, many objectives and hundreds of tactics.

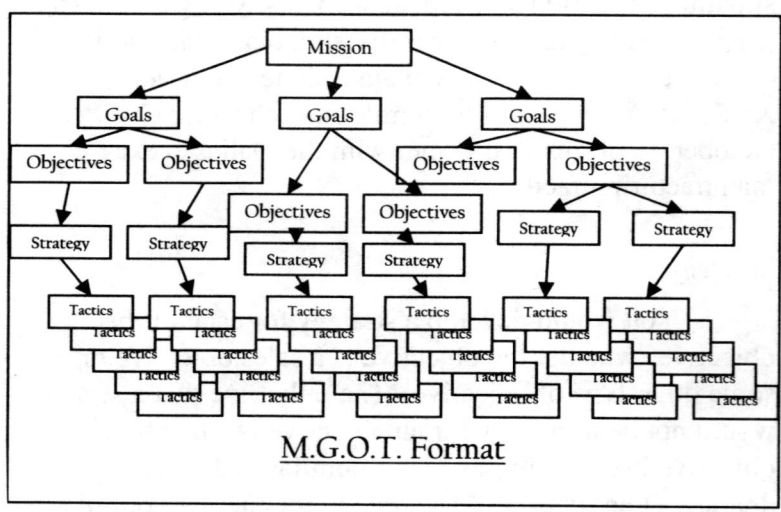

M.G.O.T. Format

Mission

The mission is the statement of purpose for the members of your team and for your company. Just like the corporate mission, this statement will define the sales team's reason for existence. For example, "We exist to service account Wiley Widgets at a world class level of customer satisfaction, achieving maximum capture of potential revenues for the mutual benefit of both Wiley Widgets and their customers." Another example could be, "Our mission is to serve customer X in the creation of unique value propositions to the benefit of their customers, their shareholders and their employees."

Goals, Objectives, Strategy and Tactics

The goals would relate directly to the account or the territory pertaining to the mission and would reflect a future position for the team. Under each of the goals, define several objectives to reach that particular goal. With each of the objectives, you will need to create a strategy, defining the approach you will take toward achieving that particular objective. Finally, with each strategy you will have tactics. As before, the tactics must support your strategy.

In complex military operations that involve multiple services, weapon systems, aircraft, ground troops, supporting infrastructure and all the other assets necessary to carry out such an operation, the planning format is substantially the same as the M.G.O.T. planning format. This planning format is what gives generals the ability to orchestrate vast quantities of resources and coordinate the most complex battle plans.

The greater the complexity, the higher up the corporate agenda you need to go. The most complex sales situations require a larger planning format. For less complex situations, you can use the smaller planning formats. In effect, you are the general of an army of colleagues and resources with the commensurate obligation to deliver results. You would never enter into a campaign without first building a plan that accommodates the scope of the sales situation.

Defensive Countermeasures

You have built your strategic plan for pursuing an opportunity that you feel is winnable and vital to your success. You have been in the early communication stages with the customer and you are about to shift your sales campaign into high gear. Your team is ready, your manager's ready, and you are feeling good about your chances of success. Before you start, spend some time thinking about what your competitors' response will be to your sales strategy. What would you do if you were in their position?

Even though you have created a strategic plan with a strategy that you feel confident in, your plan is incomplete. Your plan to this point is offensive, intended to advance your selling effort. Your plan is incomplete because you have not built in the defense. This is tantamount to entering a sporting competition with only your offensive plan without taking into account the necessary defensive maneuvers that will enhance your plan's likelihood of success.

Defensive Countermeasures are designed solely to anticipate your competitor's moves and negate them. For example, you have set up a meeting with the executives in your opportunity for the end of next week. You know that your competitor is well positioned with the lower level people. You are executing a Flanking strategy and if all goes well at the meeting, you will be changing the rules at that time. What kind of defense should you think of using before the meeting?

First, it would be a good idea to get to the lower level audience quickly to engage them in some activities that will limit their availability to the competition. You would also want to be sure that your competitor does not have an equal opportunity with the senior level audience.

Another idea might be to use pre-meeting correspondence to send the wrong message to your competitor. You want your competitor to think the agenda for the meeting is non-threatening, just another "me, too" sales campaign. You do this if you know that one or several of the senior audience are predisposed to the competitor and likely to share your correspondence. You would then arrive at the meeting and, for justifiable reasons, switch the message and the agenda.

Countermeasures are tactics that are designed to help you either gain control or maintain control of the sales campaign. They are a separate group of tactics focused on the defense of your plan. Design these tactics with intent and forethought, integrating them into your normal planning process. Countermeasures can be very effective and can be the difference between winning and losing a sales campaign. No military strategist would ever go to battle without defensive countermeasures.

In World War II, as the allied troops were staging for the continental invasion, all sorts of intelligence games were being played. The allied armies used tactics specifically designed to lead the Nazis to believe one thing when something entirely different was transpiring. One of the key factors in the success of the Allied invasion was the fact that the Nazi commanders did not believe that the invasion was going to happen down the coast in Normandy. After all, they had gathered intelligence that the invasion was actually going to happen where the English Channel was narrow, in Calais. The Germans gathered their resources, troops and guns and built their heaviest defenses at the point where they believed the invasion would come. Where do you suppose that intelligence came from?

Another clever countermeasure that confused the Nazis was the use of false tanks and aircraft. The Allies had been setting the stage where the enemy would expect them to be preparing. Using tanks and aircraft made out of inflatable rubber they set up mock bases. From the air, they looked like an invasion force staging for war.

Defensive Countermeasures, done well, are very effective tactics with the sole intention of throwing your competitor off the path, sending them in the wrong direction. They are tactics designed to give false and misleading information about your strategic intentions. They are tactics designed to make the selling effort of your competitor more expensive and less effective. This may sound like some form of illegitimate behavior. Done improperly, they can be. Done well, countermeasures are not the same as lying, cheating or some other unethical behavior.

Some companies have formal departments dedicated to studying and anticipating the competition's future actions. Years ago, it was considered unethical by most corporations, falling under the negative category called "corporate spying". Today it is called Competitive Intelligence, and it is a legitimate corporate function. The professional society known as "SCIP"- Society for Competitive Intelligence Professionals - is involved with competitive intelligence. In their code of ethics, they state that they will comply with all applicable laws, domestic and international; they will disclose all relevant information, including one's identity and organization prior to all interviews; they will respect all requests for confidentiality of information; and they will avoid conflicts of interest in fulfilling their duties. Clearly, one of the reasons for the existence of SCIP is to clean up the image of professionals engaged in this profession.

The final arbiters of whether or not a particular countermeasure is unethical are going to be you and your customer. In the light of day, will the countermeasure bother your conscience? Will the customer consider countermeasures unethical? If you have any qualms whatsoever about a given countermeasure, then do not use it; take a pass. Do not do anything that you or your customer might feel is unethical or immoral. However, you are responsible not just for the offensive aspects of your sales campaign, but also for the defense.

In the planning and the execution of countermeasures, you are anticipating two different actions from your competition. The first action required by you is an attempt to predict your competitor's moves. The second is your competitor's response to your strategic plan.

Predicting Your Competitor's Moves

In this first category of countermeasures, your intention is to negate the strategy and the tactics of your competitor. You are attempting to predict what your competitor's strategy and tactics will be in their campaign. You can never be sure, of course, what someone else's future moves will be. They may decide, at the last moment, to deviate from their normal path. Fortunately, salespeople can be predictable.

Based on what you know about your competition, you can accurately forecast what they will do. You can do this with some degree of certainty because sales organizations are creatures of habit. As human beings, when we have success doing things a particular way, we have a tendency to repeat ourselves.

For example, even though it borders on being masochistic, application software companies have had a tendency to begin their sales campaign with a demo. In many cases, they will haul in their demo, set it up in a room in the customer's building and then invite the concerned end users, the IT department and anyone else to stop by the demo. They will remain in that room sometimes for days, waiting for the convenience of their audience to make time for the demo. They do this because it is how they have sold in the past. It is almost like a bad habit. Companies with a clearly inferior offering will continue to sell in their habitual ways even when they know it will hurt their chances of winning the business.

Use your insight and the insight of those around you to predict more accurately the strategy and the tactics of a particular competitor. Find someone in your company who has competed with them in the past and interview them to predict the actions of the competitor. Find out about the sales team for the competitor through your contacts and then find someone in your company who has competed with them in the past. What you do with that intelligence is important and potentially critical to your success.

Pursue Opportunity

World-class chess players study every variation of moves and countermoves that every known master has ever made. There are books with the moves and countermoves listed with names like the "Sikorsky Jump" and the "Spassky Gambit". Master chess players will study those moves and all their potential variations that quickly run up into the millions of moves. They play them out and carefully analyze them. They do this with the sole intention of being able to predict the future moves of their competitors. How is it that a master player can predict the moves of another master? They have studied all the potential variations from a given board position and are cognizant of the best possible moves that their competitor could make.

Your Competitor's Response to Your Plan

Predicting your competitor's response to your strategy and your tactics as they become aware of them is not complicated. What would you do as you became aware of your strategy? Some companies, in their largest and most important sales campaigns, have people dedicated to anticipating their competitor's response and planning the countermeasures for those eventualities. Your strategic plan is not complete until you have taken this necessary step - planning for and anticipating your competitor's response.

Building Defensive Countermeasures

Use the "S.T.R.P." method as a prompting guide to identify areas where you might be able to employ countermeasures.

Strategy

What is the competitor's most likely strategy in this sales campaign? What are they going to be counting on to succeed? Why would the customer be compelled to do business with them? What will their theme be? What can you do to offset or negate the effectiveness of their strategy?

Tactics

What specific tactics is this competitor likely to use in the execution of his sales campaign? Can you predict any tactics your competitor might use? If so, how can you offset their effectiveness now?

Resources

The resource categories are Time, Equipment, People and Money. Does your competitor have sufficient resources to compete with you? Does your competitor have more resources than you do? In what ways can you assist your competitor to misallocate and waste his resources?

Products

Are the competitor's product offerings better than yours? Can you discredit or reposition their specific strengths, diminishing their value in the opinion of the customer? Are the competitor's product offerings weak? Can you expose and exploit their weakness to your advantage?

Applying Countermeasures

It is unlikely that your competitor will be giving as much thought to building their plan as you. Their sales campaign, nonetheless, will attempt to position their offering in as favorable light as possible. Their lack of a cohesive, well-executed strategy does not mean that they will not be effective in their selling effort.

If they are not thinking strategically, their strategy will likely emphasize one of four things: their product, their price (through initial pricing or late campaign discounting), their company's reputation or their existing relationships with the customer.

In the case of a competitor with an offering truly superior to yours, develop countermeasures designed to offset their offering's strengths, repositioning those strengths, one-by-one, as "perhaps impressive, but only as features that are nice to have." Find weaknesses in their offering that may not be evident to the customer and develop countermeasures to highlight and emphasize those weaknesses.

If your competitor's offering is initially less expensive than yours, hopefully your Customer Value Orientation approach and your value proposition will be sufficient to better position you and your offering with the correct customer audience. If not, find ways of reframing your offering as the minimum requirement for the customer to be able to derive any value at all from their contemplated purchase. If the customer were to buy something less expensive, they would be unable to derive the same economic return as they would by buying your more expensive offering.

If your competitor is likely to offer a price discount late in the sales campaign, find countermeasures that might be able to offset the effectiveness of their discount. For example, attempt to establish the suspicion with the customer that your competitor may have failed to analyze their problem properly and is only now attempting to make up for their lack of professionalism by dropping their price. "What kind of a long term partner does that make them?"

Another approach to handling a competitor who aggressively discounts is to suggest to the customer that they will have to reduce service levels in the future to remain profitable. That is, "At some point in the future if they continue to give their offering away, they'll have to reduce their service level with you, too."

Another idea is to establish with the customer that based on what you have been seeing in the other situations, they could expect a discount of 30%, even more. When the competitor shows up with only a 10% discount, the customer will naturally be disappointed.

If your competitor has fewer selling resources than you do, find countermeasures you can employ to cause their few resources to be even more inadequate. Develop an activity level in the sales campaign with the expectation of reciprocity that is unsustainable for your competitor. For example, use reference site visits, studies, white papers or other means that the customer would also expect from your competitor. You might even suggest that the customer get the same treatment from your competitor knowing that it would be difficult, if not impossible, for your competitor to keep up.

Product-to-product comparisons are the most common form of competitive intelligence available. Most companies have these available for you to use to your advantage. Use these comparisons, not only to highlight with the customer where your strengths are, but also to focus on your competitors' product or offering strengths and weaknesses. Find ways to contrast your competitor's strengths in a light that minimizes them and find ways to highlight their offering's weaknesses. Your aim here is to discredit their offering's strengths and to exploit their offering's weaknesses.

Countermeasures are those tactics that you will develop to weaken your competitor's strategy and tactics. Countermeasures are those tactics that you develop to anticipate the responses of your competitor. Your ability to play both ends of the field, both offense with your strategic plan, and defense with your countermeasures, will enable you to win more often and with less effort and expense.

Caveat

As you begin to create specific ways to counter your competitor's offerings and strategies, a measure of caution is necessary. Countermeasures have a higher possibility of backfiring on you than other aspects of your strategic plan. Be careful that the countermeasures you employ do not turn around and hurt you or your sales effort.

In placing countermeasures, you seek ways to install the countermeasure in such a way that it will be successful, it will yield the result you want and it will not come back and haunt you or your strategy later on. The placement of countermeasures is best done in those "off-line" moments with a customer, in informal types of settings. For example, lunch and dinner are informal venues. In those moments before a meeting gets started when people are just settling in, the opening moments of a telephone conversation, or as you are walking down the hall are also informal moments that are appropriate for the placement of countermeasures. These moments allow you to bring up a particular subject, allowing you to place the countermeasure.

Execution

The execution of the countermeasure needs careful thought as well. Countermeasures need to be placed in such a way that the customer is not offended by your intention. If you are too direct or too obvious in the way you go about installing the countermeasure, you run the risk of offending the customer's sensibilities. Be sure that you are placing the countermeasure in such a way that it will actually enhance your stature with the customer. They may be fully aware of your intention, which is appropriate in a competitive sales campaign, but only if you are able to put it into place in a socially acceptable fashion.

If the execution of your countermeasure is too direct, too unacceptable by the culture or standards of the customer, then your intended outcome will not be achieved. In fact, the outcome may turn on you and hurt your relationship building activities, setting you back in the sales campaign. Be cautious as you go about placing the countermeasure. Be sure that you will not offend the customer.

Finally, be careful not to detonate your own countermeasures. Keep track of the countermeasures that

Pursue Opportunity

you have put into place so that you do not pass by later on in the sales campaign and trip them yourself.

Profiling and Situation Analysis

The most critical aspect of strategic planning is the ability to gather and analyze relevant information. Your ability to analyze the information and to arrive at the essence of the information, to define the one key pathway, is critical in developing successful strategic plans. This part of strategic planning, referred to as Profiling or Situational Analysis, is the gathering and the analysis of information.

When Lee Iacocca retired from his stellar career as Chairman and CEO of Chrysler, one of the major U.S. business magazines interviewed him. When asked what he valued most in business his reply was swift, "competitive advantage". When Iacocca was pressed for his definition of competitive advantage, the reply was equally swift, "Competitive advantage is one per cent more information, one day ahead of the competition and knowing what to do with it."

As high-level selling professionals, you are hungry for, and consumers of large quantities of information resulting from your research, questions and conversations with your customers. How you analyze and employ that information and how you capitalize on that information is vital to your success. Good information, early in the sales campaign, is extremely valuable. Capitalizing on that information in a unique, professional, ethical and creative way will set you apart from your competitors.

Opportunity Profile

The Opportunity Profile will always include three different areas of information; the customer, the competition and you, including your company and your offering. Each of these areas of information is distinct in its focus. One is focused on the customer and the customer's environment, one is focused on the competition in its many potential iterations and the last is focused on you, your company and your offering.

Customer Profile

The customer profile begins with the background information that you are able to acquire from public information sources. It involves the identification of the customer's risk/value profile. It extends into the identification of the customer's KBD's and the impacts those KBD's have, or might have, on the customer's value chain. The customer profile should extend to the customer's industry and their position in it; are they a "David" or a "Goliath"? Are they at variance with their competitors? Are they struggling to become established, catch up, or are they trying to remain ahead of the competition?

Competitive Profile

The next area of information gathering is your competition. Competition comes in many forms from direct competitors who offer the same offerings as you to competitive alternatives, dissimilar offerings intended to solve the same problem. Competition also includes an in-house alternative, the potential of the customer's building their own solution.

The competitive profile must go beyond the typical perspective of product comparisons and extend to the way your competition competes. How do they typically approach a selling situation? What strategy are you likely to see from your competitor? Do they use predictable tactics? What can you expect them to say about their offering? What can you expect them to say about your offering? The complete competitive profile includes all of these things.

You and Your Company Profile

The final area of information gathering involves you, your offering and your company. Does your company have a positive operating history with the customer? Does the customer know and respect your company? Does your product or service offering meet the customer's articulated specifications? Does the customer see you personally as a unique source of value? If so, by whom and what is that perceived value?

A complete profile involves an in-depth, honest appraisal of the selling situation. It involves a close examination of your customer, your competition and yourself. High-level selling requires a candid and straightforward appraisal of the sales situation. The profile that ignores shortcomings is self-mutilating. The truthful profile, no matter how blunt, is enlightening and edifying.

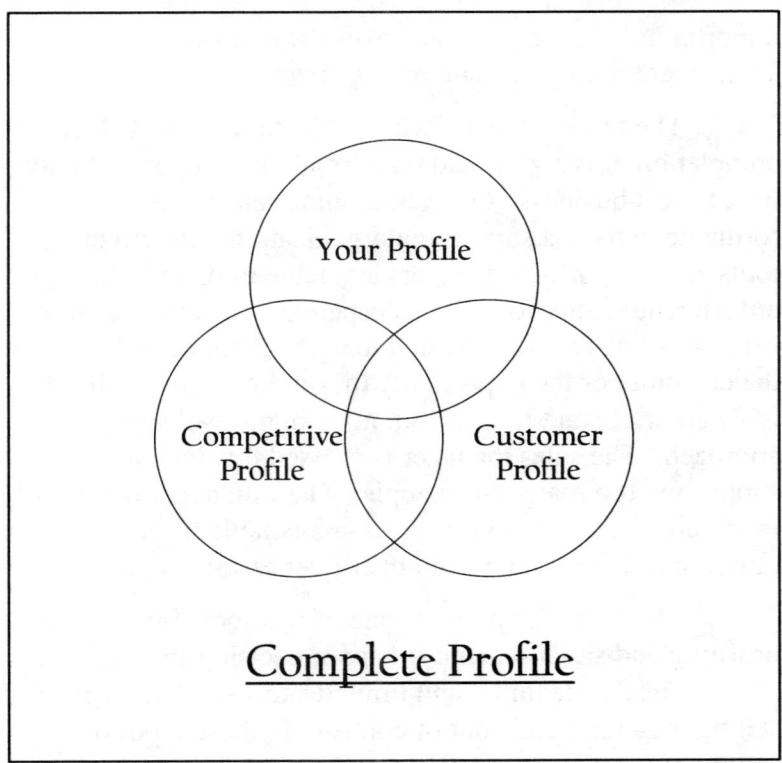

The Need for Analysis

Information and the quality of your analysis are the sources of your competitive advantage. You will seldom gather too much information. Lack of good information stifles your selling success. The collection of information requires you to dedicate time to the gathering and the analysis of that information.

Salespeople are pressured on all sides by their customers, managers, company and their personal lives. Time is a precious commodity that is typically not available in sufficient quantities to adequately profile and analyze an opportunity. This condition leaves the sales campaign insufficiently prepared and disorganized.

The tendency is to exit the planning effort before completion, relying instead on normal thinking or just plain luck to win business. Of course, some salespeople are fortunate to have a supporting organization with effective tools and supporting managers available to them. The unfortunate reality for most salespeople, however, is quite the opposite. The tools available to them are not relevant to the customer or the opportunity they are pursuing. These tools are irrelevant to a consultative, high-level sales approach. The sales manager is pressed for time, and is supporting too many salespeople. Their manager is involved in closing business and unavailable for team building or increasing the competitiveness of his people.

The result is chaos, a state of mediocre opportunity profiling and situation analysis, poor decision-making, little or no strategic planning, and limited success. This type of selling organization is out of control. In these types of selling organizations, profiling and situation analysis is the odd behavior, infrequently supported, when, in fact, it is essential to success.

When the stakes are high, in those opportunities that require success, those that are large or strategic to your company, you must spend the time necessary to gather enough good information to make your analysis and strategic plan effective. You cannot leave to chance the outcome of this type of opportunity. Not every opportunity you pursue would require this type of preparation and planning, but with those opportunities that qualify as significant for you or your company, you must spend the time to be fully prepared.

Pursue Opportunity

Profiling Formats

Pilots go through a pre-flight checklist every time they take off. No matter how many times they have flown or how familiar they might be with the aircraft, they are required to go through that pre-flight checklist.

The same should be true for your sales campaigns. You should develop some form of pre-flight checklist to make sure that everything you need to be successful is in place. Your profiling format should include everything you need to be able to analyze fully the situation, giving you the ability to build an effective strategic plan.

Opportunity Selection System

The following eight criteria are the critical areas of information that will help you build a complete profile. The Opportunity Selection System will help you more fully analyze and comprehend a complex sales situation.

You may want to add other criteria to the list that are pertinent to your customers or markets. You can further enhance the usefulness of the tool by assigning values to each of the criteria. This would help you to measure and analyze the sales opportunity more completely. This would also help you better understand your competitive status from two perspectives, the customer's perspective and the competitive perspective.

1. Mutual Value

Mutual Value is the type of value you represent to the customer. Does the customer view you as a CVO provider, focused on their business and financial success? Are you oriented toward a benefit type of proposition where you brought the customer the solution to a problem, rather than just a product? Are you feature-oriented and perceived as only a product provider?

Each of these levels of value is distinct from the other and is an indication of how well you are received by the customer. Does there exist between you and the customer a value-oriented dialog focused on the creation of a business related value proposition? Have you been able to establish a value greater than the product value? Are you received as a value provider with the senior management level of the customer?

If you have been able to establish a value-oriented dialog focused on the creation of a unique, business-related value proposition with the customer, you are in a powerful position that could give your sales campaign a higher degree of competitive immunity over your competitors. The establishment of a higher-level value-oriented dialog will also help you reduce or eliminate the need for price discounting.

Give yourself 3 points if you have been able to establish a value-oriented dialog with the customer and the senior levels are interested in the outcome of the dialog.

You get zero points if you have been unable to initiate this type of value-oriented dialog.

Give yourself minus 3 points if your competitor is engaged with the customer in this type of value-oriented dialog.

2. Offering Compatibility

Offering Compatibility is your offering's compatibility with the customer's currently articulated buying criteria. The buying criteria as currently defined by the customer and your compatibility with these criteria are the issues being addressed. Buying criteria are the specifications, both formal and informal, such as technology, price and other considerations in the customer's buying process, which the customer has identified as being important to their decision process.

It is important that you do not confuse your product superiority with offering compatibility. The customer may not be interested in buying the best offering. They may feel that price is more important than product superiority. Offering Compatibility is concerned with the buying criteria as currently defined by the customer and your offering's compatibility with those criteria.

The buying criteria may shift and change throughout the buying process. If you are not compatible at an early point in the sales campaign, it does not mean that you could not influence the buying criteria as you proceed.

Give yourself plus 3 points if your offering is clearly preferred at multiple levels by the customer. You have been receiving strong indications that your offering is clearly their preference.

Give yourself zero points if, at this point in the sales campaign, neither you nor your competitor has been able to establish any dominance with regard to the customer's buying criteria. The customer has been unable to articulate a preference and neither your offering nor your competitor's is advantaged.

If your competitor has been successful in shaping the current definition of the buying criteria, give yourself minus 3 points. Your competitor was instrumental in writing the Request for Proposal or similar document and the customer seems to rely on them for guidance. The customer's clear preference is your competitor's offering.

3. Account History

Account History refers to your current, installed base or your reputation with the customer. You are trying to determine if your history or reputation will serve as a positive or a negative. You have done work with this customer in the past that gives you a particular advantage in this selling situation.

Give yourself 3 points if you have a solid working relationship with this customer. Every obstacle that has come up in the past has been handled quickly and professionally and the customer has indicated some measure of appreciation for you. Your history with this customer is an advantage.

Give yourself zero points if your history is non-existent and your company's reputation with this customer neither helps nor hurts your sales campaign. While they know who you are, it is neither a help nor hindrance.

Give yourself minus 3 points if your reputation or history with the account hinders your selling effort. It might be that the last efforts at doing business with this customer left you with a real obstacle to overcome.

Pursue Opportunity

Alternatively, it might be that your competitor has a glowing history and more credibility with the customer. In order for you to win, you will have to prove yourself a worthy partner, properly acknowledging past mistakes and sincerely demonstrating your plan to overcome those previous mistakes.

4. Marketing Value

Marketing Value is the value that your other sales campaigns would gain by having this particular customer as a reference account. This customer's competitors think of them as a leader in their industry. They are a bellwether that other companies follow. They command the respect of other companies, even outside of their industry.

Give yourself plus 3 if the customer is widely known as a market leader. They have earned the highest respect of their competitors and the market in general. Winning business with this customer and being able to use them as a reference account will have a positive effect on other sales campaigns.

Give yourself zero points if this customer is not well known and will have no impact on your ability to sell to other customers.

In the case of Marketing Value, there are no negative points. Doing business with even the most non-descript customer does not detract from your other sales campaigns.

5. Buying Decision Process

The Buying Decision Process is the formal and informal way that this customer is going to make this decision. The Formal Buying Decision Process is made up of the steps the customer will use to come to a decision. These steps are public information and the customer will often describe them to you.

The Informal Buying Decision Process refers to the background process that is neither formal nor announced. The informal decision process might be the people who will be using the offering in actual practice or department heads that have a bearing on the offering. Another possibility is someone who has made similar decisions in the past but is now in some other part of the organization.

Give yourself 3 points if you can describe in detail both the formal and the informal decision processes. You are well positioned with the individuals involved in the formal decision process. You are also well positioned with the informal decision process.

Give yourself zero points if you have a clear understanding of the formal decision process, but only a vague understanding of the informal process. The decision process is neither favorable nor unfavorable for your campaign at this time.

Give yourself minus 3 points if you have only a vague understanding of the formal decision process and no idea whatsoever of the informal process. Your lack of understanding could be the result of having just arrived in the selling situation. It could also be an indication that the customer is attempting to keep you out of the game, spending most of their time with your competitor.

6. Senior Level Sponsorship

Senior Level Sponsorship is the visible support your sales effort has gained at the senior management or the executive levels of the customer organization. In addition to a physical presence with this audience, some of these key people are allies. The definition of an ally is a person who is willing to advocate publicly on your behalf.

Give yourself 5 points if you have the clear support and advocacy of more than one of the senior audience and if your competitor has yet to make it to this level.

Give yourself zero points if, at this time, neither you nor your competitor have any support at the senior level. There is no indication that they are attentive to this sales situation at all.

Give yourself minus 5 points if your competition has been there and has been able to establish firm support among the senior people.

7. Political Support

Political Support refers to the support you have gained from the Power Brokers and the Inner Circle, the most influential people. Their support for your offering makes your position in the sales campaign nearly unassailable, giving your sales effort some degree of competitive immunity.

Give yourself 5 points if you have connections to the powerful people in the account at the senior levels.

Give yourself zero points if neither you nor your competitors have been able to establish any political support up to this point.

You score minus 5 points if you are shut out of the Inner Circle due to their existing relationships with your competitor. You have no visibility with those powerful people and your previous efforts have met with frustration.

8. Compelling Business Issue

The Compelling Business Issue is the business issue that is causing the customer to move ahead quickly with their buying process. The customer feels compelled to act now as opposed to some point in the future. There is a particular pain or urgency connected with the contemplated purchase and the health of the customer's business is at stake.

Give yourself 5 points if the Compelling Business Issue is an urgent need, tying directly to a higher-level corporate initiative. Your offering and value are closely associated with their compelling factor. The person sponsoring the compelling factor is a powerful person.

Zero points are yours if you have not been able to identify the Compelling Business Issue, yet the customer seems to be moving ahead quickly with the buying process. At this point, however, neither you nor your competitors are associated with the Compelling Business Issue.

You get minus 5 points if your competitor is closely associated with the Compelling Business Issue and the issue is strong and sponsored by the right people.

Pursue Opportunity

Mutual Value	-3 to +3	
Offering Compatibility	-3 to +3	
Account History	-3 to +3	
Marketing Value	-3 to +3	
Buying Decision Process	-3 to +3	
Senior Level Sponsorship	-5 to +5	
Political Support	-5 to +5	
Compelling Business Issue	-5 to +5	

Analyzing the Score

If you were to put these eight factors on a spreadsheet and analyze your opportunity, looking at these criteria would give you a good analysis of the selling situation. It would allow you to determine what aspects of your sales campaign need further attention. It could point your sales campaign in one direction or another.

Looking at the total score of the eight criteria would also give you an overall look at your competitive status in the opportunity. You could use the total score at various points throughout the sales campaign to indicate whether your strategy is working or not. Looking at the total score would also enable you to forecast your business better. You could also use the total score to make resource allocation decisions. For example, if you are resource constrained and faced with three different opportunities, the Opportunity Selection System will help you decide where to best deploy your resources.

Dominant

You are dominant if your score is between 24 and 30 points. This is an indication that you are well positioned with the customer and your forecast for the business should be confident, though not assured. You are clearly ahead of the competition.

In the dominant position, you should consider either Preemption or a Head-to-Head Strategy and your countermeasures should focus on maintaining the lead and accelerating the campaign.

Limited Advantage

You have a limited advantage if you scored between 10 and 23 points. This indicates that you have a small advantage over your competitors but have not yet attained a competitively dominant position. Strategically, you may be required to use a Flanking strategy or other non-traditional approach. Defensive countermeasures should be focused at both advancing your cause and at limiting the ability of the competition to gain ground. You should anticipate desperate moves from your competitor as the sales campaign advances.

At-Risk

You are at-risk if you score between minus 10 to plus 9 points. The advantage is neither yours nor the competition's and you are at-risk to be out-positioned in the near future. Strategically, you may consider any type of strategy except the Preemption or the Head-to-Head strategy since you have no discernable advantage over the competition. You cannot afford a "me, too" strategy. Your defensive countermeasures should be focused on tripping up the competition, limiting their strengths and damaging their credibility.

Competitively Weak

You are competitively weak, if you scored between minus 27 and minus 11. The score indicates that you are out-positioned and out-gunned in every way. Except for some drastic measures on your part, you will be unable to turn this situation around to your advantage. Strategically, it may be a situation to exit unless you can do some real damage to the competition. The only types of strategies that you should not use are the Preemption, Head-to-Head or the Contain strategies. You will not be able to turn this situation around with an operational level, technical approach. Focus your countermeasures at making your competitor's win as expensive as possible.

SWOT Analysis

Frequently mistaken for a planning tool, the S.W.O.T. Analysis is actually a profiling tool. S.W.O.T. (Strengths, Weaknesses, Opportunities and Threats) is a commonly used format to build profiles that are more complete. This tool has been used frequently by military organizations to build the profile and then disseminate the relevant information to the people involved in the development and the execution of the strategic plan. It is not, however, a plan in itself, only a profile.

Use a separate S.W.O.T. for each of the areas of your profile: the customer, the competition and then yourself. A SWOT Analysis is useful in planning sessions involving the entire sales team.

You would use the S.W.O.T. analysis by putting on one "flipchart" page a windowpane box of four quadrilles. The upper left is the collection point for strengths; the upper right is the collection point for weaknesses; the lower left is the collection point for opportunities; and the lower right is the collection point for threats. You would develop one page for the customer's profile, another for each of your competitors and then a page for you and your company.

The planning session should be focused on analyzing the existing information and assigning that information to one of the S.W.O.T. pages. Understand your customer's strengths, weaknesses, opportunities and threats as well as your competitor's and your own. A positive outcome of this type of session is a better understanding of the sales situation. Since the entire sales team is involved in the session, you will develop a common understanding of the sales environment.

Another positive outcome of this profiling format is that you will be able to contrast your strengths against your competitor's strengths, giving you insight into your potential differentiator. Your differentiator should be a unique strength that is not present with your competition. If you and your competitor both have the same strength, those strengths will offset each other and would not be a differentiator for your strategy. You are looking for the answer to the strategic question, "What am I counting on to succeed?"

In your planning session, as you approach the development of your strategy, you will be able to contrast your remaining unique strengths with your customer's weaknesses and threats. This would be the answer to the other strategic question, "Why should the customer buy from me/us?" This could provide you with the unique connection between the customer's critical need and your unique strength. This is the kind of connection that you should be seeking in the development and the articulation of your strategy.

Strengths	Weakness
Opportunity	Threats

S.W.O.T. Analysis

PMI Analysis

A critical part of building a strategic plan is the analysis of information and the identification of the critical path, the strategy that becomes the most apparent and potentially successful alternative. In the course of information gathering, it is important to realize that you, at that point, are probably unaware of what information is important and what information is not.

One way of distilling vital information from the volumes of raw information is by developing tables of PMI, or Plus, Minus, Interesting. In a column labeled "Plus", list all the information that seems to be positive to your selling effort. In a column labeled "Minus", list the information that is negative and in a column labeled "Interesting", list

Pursue Opportunity

the information that seems to be vital or critical to your selling effort. Information that does not fit in any of these columns is unlikely to be important or salient to your sales campaign.

The advantage of this type of information analysis is that you can do this on your own and distill large amounts of information down to three shorter lists of relevant information. You could even assign values to each point based on your estimation of its relative importance. From the finalists, you should be able to identify what your strategy should be in the selling situation. Your focus is still to answer the two key questions, "Why should the customer buy from me/us?" and, "What am I counting on to succeed?"

Plus	Interesting	Minus

P.M.I. Analysis

Obstacle Analysis

As you go about gathering and analyzing information through whatever format is most appropriate for your particular situation, keep a list of each of the critical obstacles that are visible. Obstacles are known barriers between you and your sales objective. In most situations, you will be able to define those obstacles as you define your strategy.

Taking each obstacle one by one, determine how you will deal with and eventually overcome those barriers. What will you do to be sure that an obstacle does not derail your entire strategic plan and ultimately, derail your

Pursue Opportunity

success? Define each obstacle as an objective then define a strategy for overcoming each obstacle.

Ignoring obstacles is not an option. If you know that a particular barrier will present itself in the course of your sales campaign, ignoring it or simply hoping that it does not materialize, will not solve the problem.

For example, if your sales objective requires the approval of the related marketing organization to implement fully, but the customer's buying process specifically excludes them from the decision, ignoring the marketing organization is not a viable option. You may want to compel their involvement in the decision-making process, if possible, or you may want to anticipate their future involvement and prepare for that eventuality.

A sales team for a Fortune 100 company was competing for a service contract with a banking company. As they were developing their strategy, it became clear (by the customer's own policy) that the Board of Directors would have to give the final approval for a purchase the size of their sales objective. Any expenditure over a certain amount required the approval of the Board of Directors. An influential member of the Board had a negative experience with their company and was going to campaign against the approval of the contract.

Even so, the selling team felt that they were competitively advantaged to win the business with the established decision making process, but would likely run into stiff opposition once the Board became involved. In order to overcome this known obstacle, the selling team re-crafted their sales objective into three parts, allowing the size of each to fall below the level requiring the Board's approval. Yet, by winning the first of the three parts, they were almost assured of winning the other two parts of the contract. They won the first contract, then by default, the other two parts, and they never had to obtain the Board's approval.

There are many ways of creatively dealing with known obstacles, but you will never get the chance if you do not segregate them and deal with each one directly.

Summary

Pursue Opportunity is the way a high-level salesperson manages a competitive selling situation. It is the careful analysis of the selling situation and all the pertinent information. It is the development of an effective strategy to win the business. It is the creation of defensive countermeasures to defeat competition proactively.

The Phase III Salesperson is able to think two or three steps ahead of the competition. They are able to position themselves in the right place at the right time. They are able to gain Strategic Clarity in the midst of chaos. Using these tools and becoming a strategic thinker will help you win more business.

Relationship Management

In the execution of a sales campaign, the salesperson's ability to build and maintain personal and professional relationships with the right people is vital to success. Understanding people, their personal and professional agendas are central to Relationship Management. Being able to understand politics and the political structure in the customer organization helps the high-level salesperson create and sustain momentum.

Relationship Management

As a high level salesperson, building and maintaining professional relationships is vital to your ability to win business. How well you get along with your prospects and customers will have a lot to do with winning or losing sales campaigns. In Relationship Management, there are two different concerns. The first is your ability to connect with people and develop relationships with them. The second is politics and your ability to operate successfully in the political environment inside the customer organization.

Connecting with People

As much as anything else in selling, your ability to connect with people in a sincere and professional manner, can have a dramatic impact on your success. When asked what the single most important factor that led to their buying decision, customers most frequently answer by citing their relationship with the salesperson. It may have been the credibility of the individual, or their ability to work well with them, both being the direct result of a salesperson's ability to develop a good working relationship with the customer. Successful, high-level salespeople will often attribute their success to their ability to establish a good working relationship with their customers.

As you begin to make headway into an account, the customer's earliest perception of you is as an outsider, an unknown commodity. Their perception of you will be based on how well you are able to connect with them.

After all, you are an unknown and they have much to learn about you. In these early stages of relationship development there is an interviewing process that must take place. Does the customer need your presence and your offering? Will they be able to rely on you when things become more challenging? Are you the type of salesperson who will say anything to win the business and then abruptly move on? Your ability to quickly reassure them and move through these earliest stages of relationship development will help you leap forward past your competition.

Relocation companies (home moving companies) in the US are prone to go out and sell their services by talking about their product, delivery times and safety records. They seem to be completely unaware of what is really happening to the person who is buying the service. Their customers are uprooting their home, family and careers. They are leaving behind friends and family, schools and churches and the comfort that comes from familiarity. At the other end of the move, they will be facing new neighborhoods, friends, career challenges and many unknown factors. Moving can be one of the three most stressful points in life, along with coping with a loved one's death and a career change. Yet, the typical salesperson from relocation companies would rather talk about their product's air-ride shock absorbers. They seldom take into account what is really going on with the customer. They miss the point entirely.

Not that they could or should do anything about the prospect's plight. They can't, after all, do anything directly about the unknown future that faces people who are moving. They can, however, do something about the stress level of their prospects. They can offer ideas that will lessen the stress of children moving from one part of the world to another. They can offer ideas to diminish the stress of leaving behind friends and family and familiar surroundings. They can do this because they have been helping families move for years. Even with all this valuable experience, they would rather talk about their shock absorbers.

Understanding what is really going on with your customer gives you the ability to empathize, which gives you the ability to connect with the customer more easily and quickly. Empathy may not solve anyone's problems, but at least you will get it, you will be cognizant of what is really going on. Instead of talking about your shock absorbers, talk about issues that are of concern to the customer. You will be connecting with something that is relevant to the customer.

A key aspect of the Customer Value Orientation approach is the identification of the risks customers are facing and the ability to reduce those risks. When you are able to connect your offering's value with the customer's KBD's, you are connecting with something that is meaningful to them. The same is true at the personal level. Connecting with people in this way at the earliest possible stage involves understanding what is really going on with them personally.

Levels of Relationships

In selling, there are three distinct levels of relationships: Vendor, Trusted and Confidant.

In vendor status, you are a supplier or a prospective supplier. You are mostly unknown to them and they are unknown to you. This earliest stage of relationship is the get-to-know-me stage of the relationship where you are eager to become familiar with them and explore the possibilities of doing business. In order to move from the vendor class to the trusted class, you have some work to do.

Trusted status comes about when you have been able to demonstrate that you are worthy of their trust and you are relevant to their concerns. The information they share with you is more sensitive and their treatment of you has changed from vendor status. You are connecting with the prospect or the customer at a more personal level and the topics of your conversation are more personal in nature. They are willing to show you around their organization and they will go out of their way to introduce you to others in their organization.

Confidant status means that they are sharing with you the most intimate details of their company and their own professional aspirations. The information that is being shared at this level is not for public consumption and must be treated with the utmost care, even inside their company. They have already gone out of their way to introduce you to others in their organization and now are sharing the inside story on politics, political agendas and power.

It's unrealistic for you to believe that you can go from vendor class to trusted class to confidant simply by being there, without deliberately doing something to change their perception of you. It may be impossible to move out of the vendor class anyway, but waiting for improvements in your relationships will usually not occur without proactively doing things to make that happen. To move from one level to the next involves several steps.

First, you must understand the customer, their personal agenda and their relationship to their corporate agenda. This involves getting them to a point where they are willing to share their personal details with you, things like how many kids they have, where they live and the details of their professional background. You can't just come out and ask them these kinds of questions. It is important that they are willing to share these details. They will eventually come to the point where they would like to talk about themselves. However, forcing them to reveal their personal details to you too quickly is neither professional nor comfortable.

Some people are more willing to share personal details than others. However, with few exceptions, people do like to talk about themselves and will eventually share that type of information with you, but only after you have gained their trust.

The Personal Agenda

To move up from vendor status means that you must make efforts to understand the person at a more intimate level. To one degree or another, you will be attempting to understand your customer's motivation in life, their aspirations and their goals. You want to understand their background, their beliefs and their attitudes about life. The more you are able to learn, the better you will be able to relate to the person and not just their role in their company.

Most people have some form of personal agenda. They may or may not have their agenda well articulated and written down, but for the most part people do have aspirations and goals. You can better understand the personal agenda by using the M.G.O.T. format of the corporate agenda. People do have missions, goals, objectives and tactics, although they probably don't think of them in those terms.

For most people, a personal mission is not something that they have given much thought. Most people allow their environment or their background to determine their mission in life. Many times people do not have a clue what their mission in life really is. Their mission this year might be focused in one direction, usually established by some external force such as their work or their family. The next year, due to a change in employment or a change in their personal life, their mission might migrate to some new area.

Some people, however, truly qualify as mission driven people. These people will typically possess a strong sense of personal identity, uninfluenced by external factors. They possess a strong sense of purpose and a definite idea of who they are and where they are going.

A mission driven person is able to tell you in direct, well thought out words what their mission in life is. They can repeat it day in and day out using substantially the same words every time. Because of this dedication to their mission, they will have a tendency to change direction less often. They tend to stick to their life's mission even when things are tough. If the company they work for supports their purpose in life, the mission driven person is professionally content. If the company they work for does not support or appreciate their mission in life, they might be discontent, even closet crusaders.

They are, most often, comfortable with themselves. Because of their strong sense of identity, they will determine the agendas of the people around them. Often, their mission is altruistic in nature, meaning that their inspiration is not for their own personal gain, but the good of others. Because their mission is altruistic, other people will easily identify and be able to support their mission. For this reason, the mission driven person will shape the corporate agenda and establish the corporate values of their company.

A good example of a mission driven person would be Nelson Mandela. His mission in life was to end the government-sponsored form of racism, Apartheid, in South Africa. This became his life-long quest. This was his purpose in life in spite of his incarceration within sight of Cape Town, in spite of the persecution that he endured, in spite of the fact that few people around him thought that he would ever succeed.

If you are not a mission driven person, consider that it is the person with the strongest agenda who sets the agenda of those around them. What this means is that your mission in life is being established by the strongest people around you. Most people's calling in life is not as clear as Nelson Mandela's. Most people have a personal agenda that is unarticulated and dominated by their career, family or other similar factors.

Do not believe that simply because a person is mission driven, they will prevail. Do not presume that this person is in complete alignment with the corporate agenda. They may have a strong purpose, but it does not necessarily reflect the agenda of the company they work for. If their agenda is overridden by other, more powerful agendas, these people may find themselves out of position, out of the central thrust of their organization and professionally discontent. If they choose to stay in this situation, they will have to set aside their life's calling and adopt someone else's agenda. Their discontent will have to be controlled for the good of their organization or they may find themselves out of work altogether.

Personal agendas will often have articulated goals. Retiring by the age of 55, buying a cabin in the woods, owning a 60-foot sailboat, putting children through college are all examples of goals. It is common for many of us to have "life goals".

Objectives follow goals. They are frequently seen in personal agendas. Objectives need to be more specific and time sensitive than goals. An example of an objective might be to complete a college level Spanish course by October of this year or put the dog through obedience school before July.

Finally, personal agendas include tactics, those "to do" lists that all of us have. An example might be to get the course catalog for the local college to find out when the Spanish courses start or sign up Fido for obedience school. The tactics are much like a "to do" list or a task manager software package.

People think about their personal agenda (even though they might not use those words) on a continuing basis. Over time, the agenda might change and shift when they change companies or jobs, have children or even make new friends. It is often inspirational to see what happens to a person's agenda when they are forced to respond to personal tragedy. For example, MADD (Mothers Against Drunk Driving) is an organization that has been making a real difference in North America, heightening the awareness of the dangers of drunk driving, bringing about significant changes in the public's attitude about drunk driving and causing significant changes in the laws concerning drunk drivers. Their mission was the result of the tragic death of a teenage girl in California involved in a car crash with a drunk driver who was a repeat offender.

The Professional Agenda

The difference between a personal agenda and a professional agenda is that the professional agenda relates to the working life of an individual. The professional agenda is the overlap between a personal agenda and the corporate agenda. There are people in this world who have a job, while others have careers. Still others in the working world have quests, people like Michael Dell, Carly Fiorina, Andy Grove, John Chambers and Bill Gates.

In a well-articulated professional agenda, the mission is at the top. It articulates who the person is in the context of their professional life. Beneath the mission are goals that define where they aspire to be professionally. Under their professional goals are objectives, the practical steps they must take to move in the direction of their goals. Beneath the objectives are tactics, the daily tasks necessary to achieve their objectives. Most people do not have well-articulated professional agendas. And, as before, the person with the strongest agenda will usually establish the agenda of those around them.

The professional agenda is the area of overlap between a personal agenda and a corporate agenda. For example, if you were to compare the personal agenda of Bill Gates and the corporate agenda of Microsoft, especially in their early years, there was little difference. They were virtually identical. This overlap was his professional agenda.

This is not to say that anything less in terms of commitment is a bad thing. Many people in this world have strong, well-articulated personal agendas that have little or nothing to do with their employer's corporate agenda. In England, there are several orders of Convents that require the sisters to go out and work in the secular world. They are as committed to their calling as any other nun, but during the day, they pursue a professional agenda.

As you encounter people in your accounts, one crucial aspect of your investigation should involve understanding their personal agendas. Understanding their personal agenda will help you do two things; it will give you greater insight into the person with regard to your relationship-building activities and it will give you insight into the correlation between the corporate agenda of the organization and their personal agenda.

The person with the strongest agenda will define the agenda of the people around them. The person with the strongest professional agenda will have greater influence on the development of that company's corporate agenda. When we begin to consider the politics and political environment of a company, the people who influence the higher levels of the corporate agenda are the powerful people with whom you want to make closer, more personal connections.

In your relationship building activities, when people are comfortable sharing with you what they might not want the rest of the world to know, they are placing their confidence in your ability to treat that type of information with care and respect. They might need you to know certain things that reveal their true motivation or the problems that face them in the execution of their part of the corporate agenda or in their buying effort. By sharing this type of information, they are revealing a part of their professional agenda. This is a clear indication that they would like your assistance in dealing with their problems and challenges. This is usually an exclusive position for you. This level of sharing does not happen with just anyone.

This may sound like a good thing. It can be a powerful component of your sales campaign. However, this kind of relationship can also be a bad thing, since not all allies are equal. If the person who is sharing this level of information with you is widely perceived by their organization as anti-agenda, your association with that individual can have a debilitating, perhaps even fatal effect on your sales campaign.

Salespeople have a tendency to enter the sales situation through the door that is open. This door is typically directly associated with the operational aspects of the offering or the buying process. Even though these contact people may have a professional agenda that is in alignment with their organizations, it might not be the case. You might assume that if these people were delegated the decision-making responsibility of this particular buying process, they must be aligned with their organization and must be a powerful person. This is frequently not the case.

Experienced salespeople know that decision makers can be non-influential people. Decision makers are delegated the arduous task of wading through all the minutiae associated with the buying process, the technical specifications, the proposals and the responses. They are the ones who are responsible for the communication with the potential suppliers as well as the rest of their organization. They are not really the decision maker as much as they are technical evaluators or perhaps recommenders. Because of this, they are not concerned with the larger issues related to the purchase. Because of this relatively low-level functionary capacity, other forces in their company can veto them. They may choose you as their provider but you could lose the business anyway.

Too often, salespeople will enter sales situations intent on endearing themselves to anyone and everyone who will spend time with them. They are intent on increasing their likeability quotient with everyone they encounter. They meet people, talk to people and try to make some kind of personal connection with all of them.

The problem with this approach to relationship development is that when you do anything for anybody, you give the impression to the customer that your time and efforts are not valuable. For the agenda-driven person, time is the most valuable resource since it is irreplaceable. In addition, when you do things for people in accounts, you should have a reasonable expectation that they will do something for you in return. If you do not share your expectation for something in return, they may or may not feel inclined to reciprocate. This is an exchange of one value for another. As a high-level salesperson, you should expect a fair return for your time and efforts.

There is great value in being able to connect with people professionally. Those relationships can have a positive impact on your ability to succeed in a sales campaign. Ultimately, your relationship building activities are focused at creating a direct link between the customer's personal agenda and doing business with you. When you are successful in making that professional connection, they recognize a personal benefit. This benefit is personal in nature and has nothing to do with your offering's business or technical value.

Creating Momentum

For those of you involved in selling, the concept of momentum should not be foreign. Positive momentum is a tremendous thing to feel in a sales campaign. When you hear many supporting voices from the customer organization, particularly late in the competition, the feeling of momentum is almost palpable. Negative momentum, where even your friends will not speak with you, late in the sales campaign, is a death knell. You are not only losing, you have probably already lost the business.

The definition of positive momentum in the context of a selling campaign is to have whole groups of people emotionally engaged with the idea of doing business with you. They have crossed the imaginary boundary between contemplated and realistic and are adjusting to the idea of doing business with you and your company.

There are many hurdles in any decision-making process. Not all people involved in the decision-making process are going to have the time or the interest to do all the work necessary to come to a decision. These people rely on other people to do the evaluations and render a good decision. Some people involved in the decision process will not make a decision until they absolutely have to, and that usually will occur late in the sales campaign. As a few of the decision-leaders come to their decision in the buying process, others will follow. As others begin to follow, mass psychology takes over. Everyone begins to assume that a decision has been reached. They begin to signal the winner before the final contract is official. They actively avoid the loser. These positive and negative signs are unmistakable. Very rarely will you win without some informal signal from the customer.

As a high-level salesperson, you must take it upon yourself to create and maintain positive momentum in your sales campaigns.

Plato's Theory

Plato once hypothesized that human beings exist in three distinct realms - logical, emotional and physical. The logical universe is where mathematics, science and logic prevail. The logical mind is convinced through empirical evidence. The emotional realm does not require empirical evidence to be convinced. Emotions are dominated by feelings and intuition. The physical realm is where the logical and emotional human encounters the outside world.

We are emotional beings, making decisions sometimes based on nothing more than a whim or some other emotional response. An emotional response is a decision that something must happen, even though there may be no rational or logical reason to support the decision. While some of you may feel that emotions should have nothing to do with good decision-making, the reality is that emotions always have a role in the decision making process.

The physical or kinetic realm is the world around us, the physical things within our range of perception. We respond to our logical and our emotional selves in the physical world with physical actions.

Plato's theory suggests that nothing happens in the physical world until both logic and emotion are activated.

From our perspective as salespeople, this means that our customers will not buy until both logic and emotion are activated. Even in business, a customer's emotional state will have a lot to do with how they make their buying decisions and what they decide to buy. Emotions can even have an impact on when a customer decides to buy.

According to Plato's theory, when a person engages emotionally with the idea of buying and can logically support that decision, then they are willing to take physical action. They are ready and willing to buy. You need to understand Plato's theory, particularly the idea that the emotional realm has something to do with buying, even in the B2B world. This means that as a high-level salesperson you are responsible to logically convince and emotionally engage your customer.

Most salespeople approach customers from the logical perspective, extolling the business case, the technical case or an analytical case. Professionally, this is a good way for you to proceed. Customers need the analytical, technical and business case to justify their decisions to their own organization. You must also take it as part of your professional responsibility to engage the customer's emotions as well.

In order for you to begin to expand your value in relationship building activities, you need to understand the customer's personal and their professional agendas. Then you need to find ways to engage their emotions. By doing this, you are connecting your sales campaign directly to their emotional well-being.

Emotional Engagement

Psychologists have identified more than fifty distinct human emotions. They are love, dread, hate, pathos, humor; the list goes on. Professionally, it is best to target only two, Excitement and Disturbance.

You create Excitement by your own enthusiasm for what you do, for what you sell or, for what you can do for the customer. Excitement is created by a positive outlook and attitude. Excitement is not the silly, over-the-top sort of illogical optimism people sometimes associate with salespeople. It comes from a sincere belief in what you do for a living, what you represent and what you can do for your customers. Your optimism, enthusiasm and excitement become contagious to the people you contact and they are emotionally affected by it.

Disturbance is a good approach for a high-level salesperson. Disturbance is the emotional state where customers come to realize that their current state is not what it should be to compete effectively or handle some kind of risk. Disturbance, in psychological terms, is cognitive dissonance, the moment when customers emotionally register their risk exposure. In that moment of problem-acceptance, the person is in an emotional state. The opportunity for you to be embraced by the customer happens in that moment of realization.

Setting Gap

Setting Gap is a process that you deliberately set in motion to cause a prospect or a customer to become emotionally disturbed. The desired outcome of Setting Gap is to compel customers to rewind their buying process, to destabilize the customers' decision-making process and to compel customers to reconsider the premise on which they are making the buying decision.

Setting gap is done by providing customers with an academically based assessment of their current state and then comparing that to the best-in-breed or a future state. Done well, this disturbs the customer emotionally. By convincing customers of their poor position and providing them with a vision of a better future state, you create the opportunity to position your company and your value proposition in a very compelling light.

Use great care in Setting Gap. It is a serious technique that you would use to change the customer's current buying criteria and establish your offering.

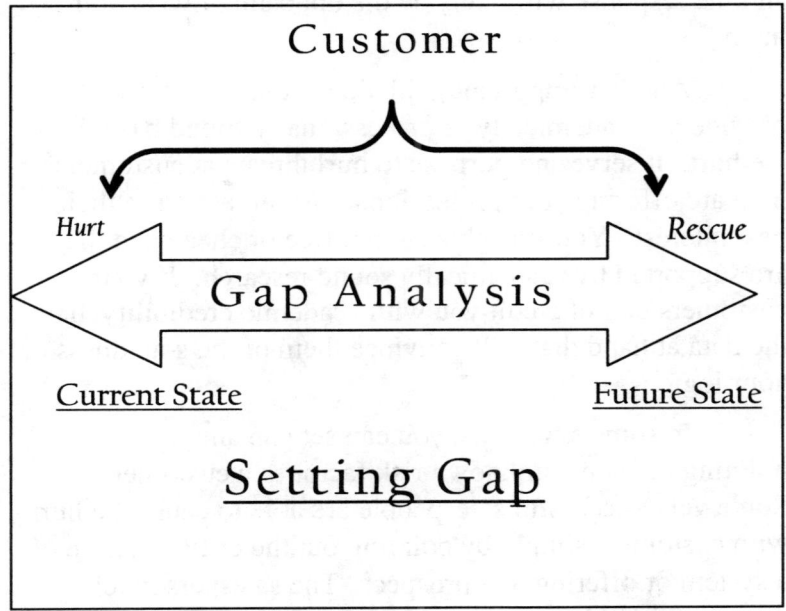

Setting Gap Guidelines

The first guideline is never to disturb or hurt the customer without the rescue immediately at hand. It is not profitable for you to bring customers to a state of disturbance and then leave them there without giving them the solution. If you do not have the solution immediately available, it means that you miss the opportunity to position your value. "Here's the hurt; I'll get back to you with the rescue in a week." You must take great pains to avoid this situation.

The second guideline is to take care not to hurt the same audience too often. In psychology terms, conditioning takes place with repetition. When you set gap with the same audience too often, they become conditioned and the response will likely be the opposite of what you intend.

Another important guideline is that you must provide an academically or professionally sound basis for the hurt. It serves no purpose to hurl threats at customers. You are offering your professional insight, acting in their best interest. Your insights are not free or cheap and they are supported by academically sound research. If your customers do not credit you with academic credibility, have the data at hand that will convince them of the soundness of your logic.

In some situations, you can set gap simply by pointing out some unknown risk factor to a customer. Some very successful salespeople are able to cause the hurt with customers simply by pointing out the critical nature of a system or offering to a prospect. The salesperson tells them in fairly blunt, but credible and professional terms, that if the customer does not have a disaster recovery plan (as an example) then they might as well close their doors. This is accomplished the same way as Setting Gap, delivered credibly, causing an emotional response in the customer. The rescue is available and offered at just the right moment.

You are responsible to sell from a logical and an emotional perspective. You are responsible for creating an emotional reaction. If you do not, you are not selling the whole customer and you miss the opportunity to create momentum for your sales campaign.

Power and Politics

There should be no question that politics has a bearing in the selling environment. Politics is a fact of life. In every sales situation, in every organization, there is an invisible structure of power and influence, organized by invisible lines and personal relationships. This structure is comprised of people, relationships, agendas and power. It is an invisible structure of walls and avenues, of competing factions and cooperating common interests.

Politics is comprised of people and relationships, dotted lines and alliances. Politics is the back-room machinations of trading this for that, of making deals to support or oppose various initiatives. It is the ability of the mighty to get things done with only a suggestion or a hint. It is the game of powerful people, people who have something to gain or to lose, something to trade. Political activity determines the corporate agenda of an organization and has everything to do with the buying process. Politics is how decisions are made, the values by which organizations operate and most important to every salesperson, with whom they will and will not do business.

There is no question that relationship building is vital to your success in a sales campaign, but are you building relationships with the right people? Are you building relationships with the people who have the power and ability to genuinely advance your selling efforts? Or are you, like many salespeople, simply trying to build relationships with anyone who will spend time with you?

Politics Defined

Politics is the ability of one person to influence another person. Politics is the presence of power or influence. Politics is the environment of personal relationships and each person's relative ability to influence the activities and agendas of other people.

The essence of politics is power. It is the ability of an individual to cross into other departments and compel other people to do things on their behalf. At the center of politics are relationships where powerful people share their power with other people in order to advance their agenda.

Politics is invisible except for brief moments in time. Politics is not a formal, published org chart. Politics is informal. Politics is competitive in nature, pitting groups of people against each other in the struggle for power, prominence and recognition. Politically sensitive information is scarce and only shared with people who have earned the right to possess the information and can be trusted to handle it properly.

The Problem with Politics

Most people do not like politics or the concept that politics has an impact on who wins and who loses. It is disturbing to many, that merit and good work do not determine who wins, loses, rises or falls. It seems that the old boy network lives on, seeming to limit others' ability to succeed. Politics seems unfair, duplicitous, deceitful and dishonest. For these reasons, the mere mention of politics frequently causes negative reactions in people.

Whatever your attitude is about politics, the first thing you need to recognize is that politics is a fact of life.

Anytime people organize into groups or companies, they will endeavor to agree on common goals and objectives. People will begin to form alliances and relationships with other people who may or may not be able to help them advance their agenda. Politics is a natural consequence of human nature.

It is interesting to watch politics played out on some of the confrontational, reality based television programs such as "Survivor" or "Big Brother". The participants create alliances, relationships motivated by common goals, to counter opposing forces. You see those alliances evaporate behind the scenes when an individual's personal goal supercedes the common goal. They divide into sub-groups and alliances with the intent of advancing some common good, but when it suits someone's personal aim, they throw out their partners to advance themselves. The competition seems to bring out the worst in the participants.

These shows demonstrate an unfortunate consequence of politics. It is seems that seldom does the most worthy or likable participant win. The same is true in companies; the most worthy opponent does not always win. If you compare companies to those reality-based game shows, it seems that the most worthy player rarely wins.

As human beings, we have a natural aversion to politics, political competition and the winners and losers it produces. The question is why, if most of us have such an aversion to politics, does political competition exist? Why do people compete with one another for power and position? Many companies have policies to establish some higher form of fairness, to offer equal opportunities to succeed or fail. There are formal reviews, grievance procedures and all manner of policies whose intention is to procedures and all manner of policies whose intention is to create a more fair and equitable environment. But, people being people, politics always seem to prevail, particularly at the higher levels of an organization.

Most people are not comfortable when others control their agenda. Most people feel that they are out of control when others exercise power over them. Many people seek power or control and, in so doing, run headlong into the agendas of other people. The person with the strongest agenda sets the agenda for those around them. Along with their talents, these people frequently emerge as leaders in their companies and, depending on their level of political ability, frequently end up at the top of their company.

There are millions of people who do not seek this type of power, who do their work, day-in and day-out, not seeking anything greater than formal compensation for their work. They seem to operate outside the forces in the political environment that surrounds them. However, businesses are not run entirely inside formal org chart structures. Much of business is done between the lines, crossing departments and functions, combining the interests of several formal functions. Especially in larger, more complex sales situations, when the proposed offering is multi-faceted, touching many different departments and many different levels in a company, the nature of the buying process is highly political in nature.

Even though many people do not like it when politics play a role in an outcome, people compete politically all the time. They seek more power and control and this limits the power of others. Alliances are formed and broken, partnerships created and blown apart, exposing the tawdry nature of partisan politics.

One reason many of us have a problem with politics is that it is duplicitous in nature. In business, it is not acceptable to seem too political. It is necessary to seem democratic, fair, impartial, evenhanded and equitable. So, as the competition for more power is waged behind the curtain, it must have the outward appearance of fairness and equanimity. Powerful people seek greater control on the corporate agenda and must do so in a seemingly fair and just manner. Politics is a way of life and more common than many of us care to think.

As a professional salesperson, you cannot opt out of politics. You cannot sit outside the political arena and claim the position of an apolitical participant. You are, by your very presence, a participant in the political struggles of your customer organization. There will be people in your selling situations that are opposed to your offering and people who might favor your offering. If customers are determined to advance their buying agenda, as a high-level, professional salesperson, you have no choice but to participate in politics. Simply by being there, you become a willing or unwilling, witting or unwitting game show participant.

If you insist on not participating in the political struggles that are consequent to your presence, you are being irresponsible. You are irresponsible to your own company and irresponsible to the people in the customer organization that would support you. Those customers supporting your offering will be fighting an internal battle on your behalf and if you are unaware of their struggles or unwilling to engage in those struggles, then you are derelict in your responsibilities.

Winners and Losers

People are people. We each have our own agenda. Given professional aspirations, people will grapple with every obstacle they see lying between themselves and their goals. They seek out and destroy. They remove obstacles. They attempt to defeat all who might, right or wrong, stand in their way. Some people are more adept at this than others. Nevertheless, especially in business, there are few who do not have an agenda to advance, a position to take or a political opinion to offer. Due to the competitive nature of politics, as with any competition, there are winners and losers.

Some people have a more heightened sense of politics than others do. There are in every company, individuals who always seem to know what is going on, who always seem to be in the right place at the right time. They may not necessarily be the most powerful person. Nevertheless, their ability to recognize the shifts in the political tides more quickly than others is what tells them where to position themselves for the next political wave.

This political acumen is apparent in some people and not apparent in others. Still others have no political acumen at all. They seem to say the wrong thing at the wrong time, invariably crossing some invisible line. There are those whose principles, their sense of right and wrong, cause them to be "out of sync" with the political structure of their companies. There are times when every person must stand up and advocate for their beliefs, not allowing others to cross certain lines without paying a price. Unfortunately, must rely on your own beliefs, weighing each situation with the care necessary to act appropriately.

Whether you like it or not, whether it offends your sensibilities or not, politics is a high-stakes game that affects your success in sales. You must always be cautious and work to understand the political environment as much as any other aspect of your sales campaign. Your first responsibility in politics is to be a detective, understanding the political landscape. Then, when it is appropriate, you can act on your observations, your instincts and your beliefs.

> ## Detection First
>
> "Recognize the fortunate so that you may choose their company and the unfortunate so that you may avoid them. Misfortune is usually the crime of folly, and among those who suffer from it there is no malady more contagious. Never open your door to the least of misfortunes, for if you do, many others will follow in its train…. Do not die from another's misery."
>
> Baltasar Gracián, 1601 – 1658

Your first responsibility in the political arena is to be a detective. You must detect who has and who does not have power. Most times, it will not be the decision maker; it will be others inside the customer organization that may not be apparent early in your sales campaign. It must be a deliberate part of your sales campaign to determine, as early as possible, who are the most powerful people.

After you enter an account, instead of thinking about who will spend time with you, your first priority should be with whom would you like to spend time? To whom do you want to represent value? Who in this selling environment has the power and the clout necessary to give you the ability to take greater control?

Political Stature

When thinking about politics, you begin to recognize that there are insiders and outsiders, winners and losers. It may seem uncaring or unprofessional to some that people may be labeled winners and losers. Like it or not, this is the nature of politics. What you are looking for is the ability of one person to compel another person to do something without having the formal authority to do so. Business schools are beginning to recognize and measure this phenomenon. It is the concept of power, the ability of a person to get others to follow by means other than formal authority.

Power and Authority

Authority is a person's formal position in his company. It is the box on the org chart and the allocation of corporate resources that goes with the box. It is a title that can be printed on a business card. It carries with it a formal responsibility of some measurable output.

The concept of power is not a formally allocated attribute. Power comes from two things; the value a person brings to the organization and the recognition of that value by the right people in the organization.

Power's Source: Public Acknowledgement

Millions of people, all over the world, go to work and provide value. It is their job and the relative importance of that job to their organization, among other things, that will determine things like compensation, stature and cultural relevance. In exchange for the value people provide through their assigned functions, they receive a paycheck. This is the transaction we all expect in exchange for our professional endeavors. It is the primary transaction.

Power does not necessarily rise from this primary transaction unless the already powerful people in the organization recognize the value provided. It is the recognition by these already powerful people of the value provided that begins to create and develop into a person's level of power.

Authority, the formal mantle of power, does bring with it a measure of power, but unless that power is useful outside of the immediate, formal area of control, then this person is not powerful. There are many senior managers and executives whose power is less than their level of authority. They fill a box on the org chart. They have a formal allocation of resources, but in the execution of their position, they are subservient to other, more powerful people. Others set their department's agenda.

As you begin to work with your accounts, you are seeking to identify who is powerful and who is not. A person's power comes from authority and the use of their authority to shape and drive the organization around them. Power also comes from a person's association with other powerful people.

Political Roles

The person with power and authority is a Powerful Authoritarian. A Powerful Authoritarian is able to exercise influence outside of their formal area of control. They are able to move across organization lines to other departments and exert influence. They are able to compel departments not under their formal control to change their priorities, to change their agenda.

Power also comes from association with these Powerful Authoritarians. This person is a Powerful Non-Authoritarian and because of their association with a Powerful Authoritarian, they have influence. They can move from one formal area of a company to another, exerting influence to reshape priorities and agendas. The Powerful Non-Authoritarian is the instrument of influence for their Powerful Authoritarian.

The Powerful Non-Authoritarian is usually invisible to outsiders. People in their own organization are aware of the Powerful Non-Authoritarian's influence. As an outsider, however, you would not be able to recognize them immediately. You may unwittingly, be working in opposition to this person's agenda before you are aware of their power.

There are people in companies that have a high and lofty title, but who have little or no influence. These people are Powerless Authoritarians. They could be the Vice President of a nonessential department, caretaking a function that is not core to their company. They could even be CEO's who are "resting and vesting", waiting for their stock options to vest before sailing off into the sunset. They could be the owner of the company whose senior staff has proven capable and whose focus has moved to other areas of interest.

The Powerless Authoritarian is also invisible, as is the Powerful Non-Authoritarian. It is not immediately evident that a particular Vice President, for example, is not an influential player in their company. Good relationships with senior people are valuable in any case, since the quality of their insight and information is much better than lower level, operational people.

The last type of person is the Powerless Non-Authoritarian. These people have no title or lofty office and they have no relationship with the Powerful Authoritarians in their company. This group of people is the largest of the four categories of people. Most people in companies are Powerless Non-Authoritarians.

Your early detection activities will focus on the identification of the Powerful Authoritarians and the Powerful Non-Authoritarians. These people are the Power Brokers and the Inner Circle, the center of power and influence in companies. These people shape the corporate agenda at the highest levels. These people operate in broader areas than just their formal office. These people are the ones who make things happen.

You must actively seek out these people, identifying them early and understanding their agendas. In that way, you will come to realize what your value could be to the Power Brokers and the Inner Circle. Your first responsibility is to be a political detective, understanding who is and who is not a Power Broker or member of an Inner Circle.

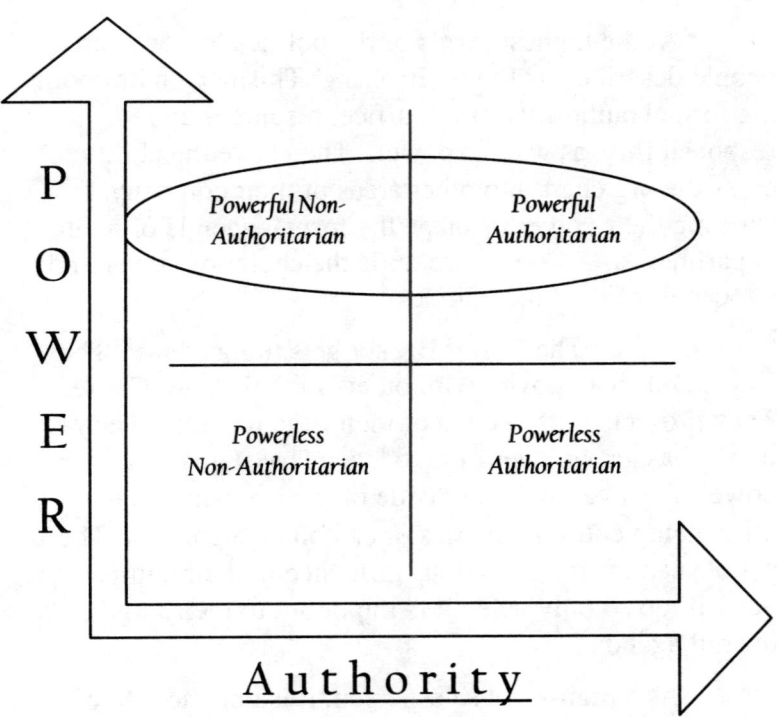

Power Brokers and the Inner Circle

At the highest levels of the political order, there are people described as Power Brokers. This person has both the formal authority of title, office, resources and responsibility, as well as power. They have the ability to cross the org chart into other areas of their company, exerting their power to shape the formal agenda of other departments. A Power Broker is the center of power and the center of the Inner Circle.

The Power Broker gets things done. They create and share power with others in their Inner Circle. They prosecute the agenda of their organization. Their power has grown over time to legendary status and their power may even spread outside of their organization, influencing entire industries or customer segments. These people can exert tremendous influence in their companies, but will do so only when it is important to their larger, overall agenda.

As a high-level salesperson, it is not enough to identify the Power Brokers in your customer's organization. Your ultimate objective is to be recognized by the Power Broker as being a member of their Inner Circle. They and their Inner Circle will realize gains greater than product or business value by doing business with you.

Power Brokers

Power Brokers are the center of influence and power in their organization. They are typically astute, political operators who, over time, have collected enough clout to enable them to set policy and act in exception to it.

They have the power to be able to make the rules, create and move budgets, develop new corporate initiatives and establish new departments. Their influence is focused on the highest levels of the corporate agenda, the mission and the goals. They also establish the cultural values of their company.

Power Brokers will most often have very strong personal and professional agendas. They possess a strong sense of purpose and direction. There is a strong correlation between their personal agenda and the corporate agenda of their company, making their professional agenda very strong. This is because the focus of their influence is on shaping the corporate agenda, moving their corporation in the direction they feel to be most important.

In spite of the Power Broker's power, they would typically prefer to influence others within their company in an indirect fashion. As they operate in their company, part of their focus is outside of their formal area of control, their area of direct responsibility. As they move around the rest of the company, they would rather operate in an indirect, more discreet fashion. If they have to operate in a direct fashion, they are careful to avoid the perception of being too political, or too overt in their actions. If they operate too overtly, they will spend their currency in a way that may be costly for them. They may achieve their objective, but in the process, they may also make enemies.

Power Brokers are careful when they choose to influence their organization. They are wise in the dispensing of their power. They will guard it and use it for the struggles that are worthy and necessary. They choose their battles wisely. They will not spend their power on lesser issues, where they could surely win, because the cost in their ability to influence future struggles might be impaired.

The Inner Circle

Surrounding every Power Broker is a tightly knit group of people connected to each other called the Inner Circle. These people are connected to the Power Broker by invisible lines with personal relationships and high levels of loyalty to each other. Others recognize them as powerful people in their company. They are able to cross organization lines and operate outside the normal lines of authority. They do so with the blessings and support of the Power Broker.

In the complex social structure of companies, these people are associated with the Power Broker and have greater input into the operation of their company than their peers. It is conceivable that these people can even compel higher-level co-workers to change direction due to their relationship with the Power Broker.

It is through the Inner Circle that a Power Broker is able to operate indirectly. The Inner Circle becomes the instrument of contact of the Power Broker with the rest of the organization.

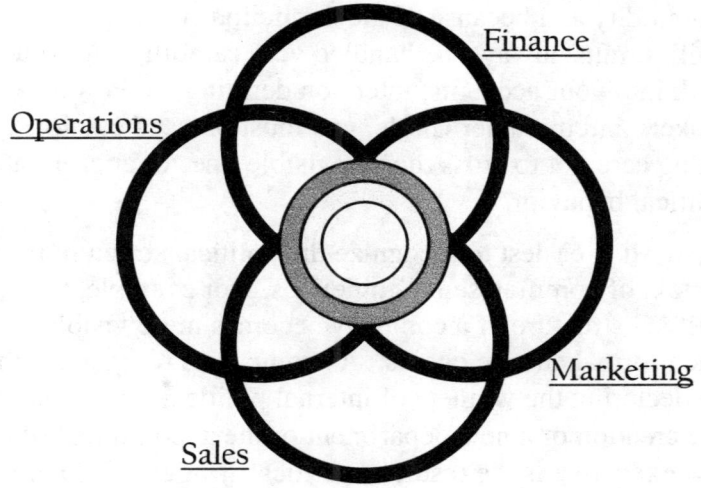

The Inner Circle

Identifying the Political Structure

Power Brokers and the Inner Circles are sometimes difficult to recognize. Political information is a scarce commodity and because of the duplicitous nature of politics, must always, be handled very carefully. As you work into your accounts, intent on defining the Power Brokers and the Inner Circle, you must proceed cautiously, taking care not to cross those invisible lines of appropriate political behavior.

It is easiest to recognize the political structure in the context of common sense guidelines. For example, the political structure of a company becomes more visible when formal change occurs. As companies reorganize, they are declaring the winners of internal political struggles. The creation of a new department or the appointment of a new executive is the result of political struggle. You are observing, unveiled, the political winners and, just as important, the political losers.

Another example of an opportunity for recognizing political structure is a change in their budget. When asking a particular department to forfeit some of their formally allocated budget, they are being re-prioritized in their organization. One department gains budget while other departments lose. This form of corporate priority setting is a visible sign that the function and the people involved have just gained or lost stature within their company.

Watching people being promoted to higher positions, you are visibly observing the results of previous political maneuvers that offer insight into the political structure. Typically, when a person is advancing rapidly up the org chart, it is because of their acknowledged value to the organization. But, as we already know, the winner is not always the most worthy. Who is supporting the individual racing up the org chart? What value does he/she provide that has made them indispensable? The answers to these questions will give you valuable insight into the political structure of the organization.

Power Brokers and Inner Circles can be found throughout companies. They are present in the departments and divisions of companies. They are present at the highest levels in companies. The larger and more complex the organization, the more you will find interconnected Power Brokers and Inner Circles.

Some powerful people will have nothing whatsoever to do with certain kinds of issues. A Power Broker from the engineering side of your customer may have little to do with the marketing efforts of the organization, but everything to do with product development. A Power Broker from the Corporate Finance area may have much to do with virtually every issue the company faces. They may show up at meetings that have little to do with finance and will exert their influence on matters that concern a broad range of issues.

As you move around your account trying to recognize members of Inner Circles and Power Brokers, be careful of the pitfalls of the naïve political operator. Beware of the fallen people who are anti-agenda in your accounts. These people seek allies for their views in spite of the negative direction they pursue. It is easy to become identified with these people because they will seek to enlist your support. If you become identified with them, your selling efforts will be debilitated.

Do not presume that because a person inside your customer organization has influence on you that they are influential. Just because they influence you, does not mean they have influence inside their company. These kinds of people will ask too much. They expect you to do things for them that might not be pertinent to your sales effort. The fact that they try to influence you unduly may be an indication that they are actually powerless inside their own company.

The power to say "No" to you and your selling effort is available to everyone inside the customer organization, even the powerless. A powerless person, who is not connected to the corporate agenda, could unnecessarily stall your sales campaign just by saying, "No".

Political Activity

Political activity is the constant of any organization. When you work in any account, you enter into an arena of perpetual conflict. Political activity is typically extracurricular activity, meaning that it is not a part of anyone's job description or part of their formal activities. Positive political activity eventually becomes part of a formal company-related agenda. Negative political activity will never become part of the formal agenda. Some political conflict becomes a priority on the corporate agenda while other conflict is insignificant. Some political conflict is motivated appropriately for the good of the organization while some political conflict is motivated to the detriment of the organization.

It is inevitable that you will become, knowingly or unknowingly, involved in the political conflicts occurring in your accounts. You may be unaware of the conflicts at first, but the more you work with the account, the more you begin to recognize those points of political conflict. It is imperative that you recognize political conflict as early as possible in your experience with an account. It is imperative that you understand the motivation for the conflict before you take sides or are unwittingly associated with the wrong side.

The reason this is vital is that some political conflict is good and some political conflict is bad. If you become associated with the wrong side of a sensitive issue, your ability to succeed in that account drops to zero. In addition, if what you are trying to sell could be a high priority on the corporate agenda of the customer, but you are associated only with the lower level, politically unconnected, your ability to take a higher level of control in the selling situation will be severely limited. It will be nearly impossible for you to achieve any political stature in the account.

Political Motivation

Political activity initiates as the result of someone's personal or professional agenda. Perhaps someone feels their company needs to develop some new department or formal job to handle some recurring problem, or someone feels their company needs to launch a new product or enter a new market. Business language is the justification of political ambition.

Recognition is a common political motivator. Receiving public acknowledgement for the value of a person's contribution to their organization is recognition. A person is trying to get something done that they feel is important. They are looking for more recognition and resources. By gaining recognition for their efforts, they may be able to gain the needed resources or gain the appreciation of the powerful people in their company.

In a selling situation, you can do things from outside the customer organization that would be inappropriate for someone inside. You can help someone gain the recognition of powerful people in their organization.

Be cautious of those that are notably against the visible corporate agenda. These people are either resistant to change or they are outside the mainstream of their own company. Their motivation is anti-agenda and their personal agenda is in direct conflict with the corporate

Relationship Management

agenda of the company. This type of motivation is seldom good and for you to become closely associated with this type of agenda can be terminal for your sales campaign. This person may be a victim of previous political activity and has found himself distanced from the center of power and now is campaigning to undo previous change. These people, with the altruism of a martyr who is doing the right thing, will seek anyone's support and actively create opportunities for failure for the new corporate direction.

Always avoid the people or the groups of people who are anti-agenda. Their poison will contaminate you, your attitude and, once discovered, will annihilate any chance you may have to win your sales campaign.

Building a Political Plan

To this point, our entire discussion about politics has dealt with detection. Who is and who is not a member of the Inner Circle? Who is and who is not a Power Broker? What is their political motivation? However, to the high-level salesperson, it is appropriate to become a deliberate participant in the political environment of the customer. You would do this only when you have sufficient verified information and you would do it with obvious caution.

In building and executing a political plan, you must proceed with the greatest caution. The components of a basic political plan are similar to a basic strategic plan with one addition, the political target. The goal of the political plan is the outcome you seek for the political target. The strategy describes the means by which you will achieve the goal, then tactics to support the strategy.

Political Target

The political target is the person who will be the center of your political plan. In selecting your political target, be sure they are aligned with your sales objective. It is important to know your political target well enough to know their personal or professional agenda and that their agenda is in alignment with your sales objective.

The political target of your plan is the person that you have identified as being most useful to your selling effort, who has a compatible personal or professional agenda. This person is not necessarily a Power Broker or even a member of an Inner Circle. It could be someone with a compatible agenda who is seeking a more prominent role or position inside the organization.

Political Goal

The goal is the outcome you want for your political target. It is not like a sales goal or objective; it is not to sell something. The political goal defines in general terms what it is you want to achieve for your political target. You might want to have your political target invited to participate in the work of a committee studying the financial impact of your value proposition. You may try to gain better proximity for your political target with a particular Power Broker in the account.

Political Strategy

The strategy of your political plan is distinct from your strategic plan. With the political goal in mind and the profile of the political environment, what can you do, from outside their company, to help advance your political target's agenda? How will you go about achieving your political goal? Often, as an outsider, you are appropriately able to do things that an insider could not. It might be that they cannot appropriately seek the acknowledgment of a Power Broker because that type of behavior is not socially acceptable in the organization. It could be appropriate for you to help.

Political Tactics

Tactics are the physical activities that you are going to use to implement your political strategy and advance toward your goal. This would include things like phone calls, meetings, studies that might lend credibility to your political target or any number of other possibilities. As an outsider, you may not be subject to the same cultural norms and behaviors as an insider. However, you cannot be too overt in the execution of a political plan. Be clever and be covert.

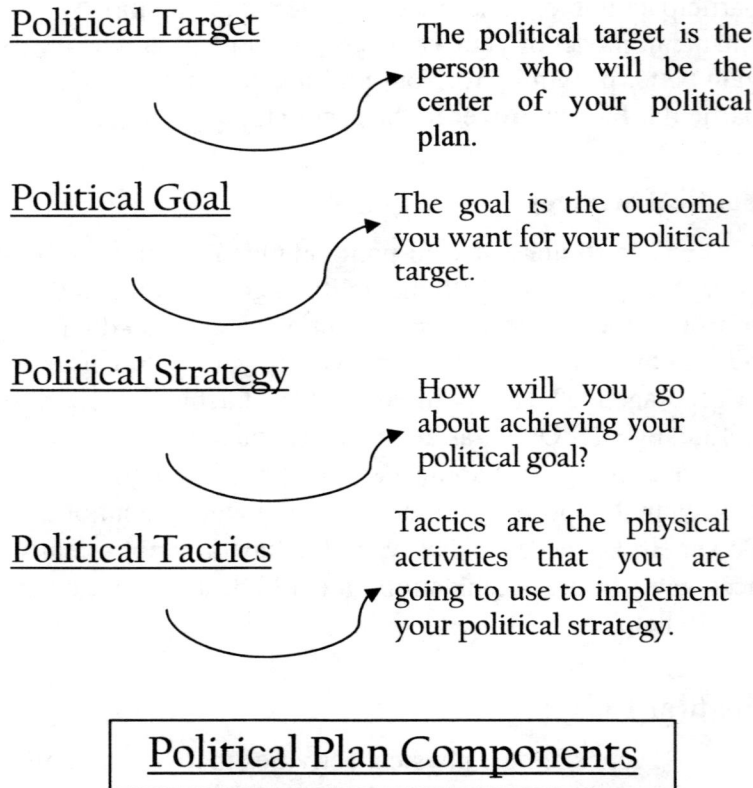

Political Plan Components

Summary

In Phase III, high-level selling, Relationship Management is pivotal. They must create professional relationships, not only at the senior levels, but also with the powerful people. They must be able to engage the personal and professional agendas of people, creating positive momentum for their sales campaigns. They must be able to determine who is and who is not a powerful person. Finally, the Phase III salesperson must be able to build and execute a political plan, advancing the agenda of their political target, and do so in a professional and ethical way.

Epilogue

Executive Evangelism

It is the bane of every U.S politician. Making solicitation telephone calls, even between elections, is something that must be done to raise the millions necessary to wage a credible, media-based political campaign. Al Gore was under investigation for making solicitation calls from his office in a government building. It has been reported that Bill Clinton, even as President of the United States, made ten or twenty of these calls every day. George Herbert Bush made thirty to forty calls a day to keep in close contact with a thousand of his friends and associates.

Just as missionaries are sent out by their churches to spread the gospel and win lost souls, a portion of your responsibility as a professional salesperson is to evangelize, to spread the word to your target audience. You cannot expect to meet with any satisfying success without spending time cold calling, in outreach mode.

For some of you, the task is pure drudgery. You are, after all, a professional, and cold calling is not exactly the epitome of professional behavior. It is not the sort of thing that most people enjoy doing, calling strangers and pitching their offering. Unfortunately, without making the investment in this type of activity, your business is not going to grow.

Even if you are responsible to only one account, as a national account manager or a global account manager, it is still necessary to spend some of your selling time in outreach mode. You may approach it differently, relying on introductions and networking with your contacts in the account. However, in the absence of a consistent program of cold calling, networking or outreach, the odds that you will grow your business are very small.

Part of the problem salespeople have with cold calling is the rejection that they inevitably encounter. Getting through to the intended prospect is difficult at best, and often seems impossible. There is a higher probability that if you made a call to a stranger as Bill Clinton or George Bush your call would be received and not screened by an admin or secretary. If they heard, "Hello, this is the President of the United States calling for Fred Flintstone…," they would be likely to take the call.

Normal Practice

Make cold calling and networking a part of your daily routine. Every day that you go to your office, you have a list of daily tasks. These are the things you do everyday; handle e-mail, check voicemail, contact colleagues, check on the progress of problems, update your current opportunities. Make prospecting a part of this daily routine. Set aside the same time every day to make only out-going, prospecting calls. Whatever your needs are for developing new business, take the time necessary to make these calls.

Just as with anything in life, there are good ways of doing things and bad ways. There is the "I don't know who you are and furthermore, I don't care, unless you'd like to buy something from me" type of cold call. Only three things matter in cold call solicitation. Will they buy? Will they buy now? Will they buy from me?

This is not the province of the high-level professional salesperson. There is a difference between cold call solicitation and high-level cold calling. Furthermore, if your approach sounds like the "I don't know; I don't care" type of call, then you deserve what you will get; they will hang up.

Your approach must be different, must stand out. It must set you apart from the other hundreds of solicitation calls that customers receive. You must demonstrate your professionalism and your credibility. You must demonstrate a genuine level of empathy for the customer. You must offer the potential of a financial gain. At the highest levels, cold calling is not a numbers game; it is a game of quality and content, sincerity and evangelism. At the highest levels, you must do your research before you ever pick up the phone.

Customer Oriented Evangelism

The customer must be the center of your outreach. You must orient your messages to the needs and concerns of your prospects. If you do not, the customer will perceive you as a product-pitching box-shifter, interested only in selling the offering and moving on. Of course, at certain levels and with certain kinds of offerings, this is acceptable behavior. Some salespeople still are required to do this type of solicitation; you find them, you sell them, and then you move on to the next one. However, this is not acceptable behavior for a professional, customer value oriented salesperson.

You communicate with prospects with a professional empathy that clearly shows that your primary interest is in their success. You communicate with language that demonstrates that you have done your research. Before you place the call, you know what is most important to them and you are ready to answer three key questions. What is in it for them? Why should they listen to you? What business impact would come from doing business with you? If you cannot answer these basic questions in the first few seconds of the call, and answer them in a customer-oriented, compelling, professional manner, then they have the right to hang up on you.

Advantages of Calling High

The ideal audience for your customer value oriented message is a higher-level manager or executive level person. It is the nature of the value oriented approach. The language you are using is not compelling at the lower, operational levels since they are primarily concerned with the execution of their part of the corporate agenda. The higher-level audience is able to appreciate and evaluate your value oriented message.

Unfortunately, the higher-level audience is generally less available for this type of call. They and their staffs are sensitized to the hundreds of unwanted nuisance calls they receive. Getting through to this audience is difficult. However, before you give up on the idea of calling the higher-levels, consider the advantages of high-level cold calling.

Immediate Results

When you call high and get through, you gain proximity to power and authority. These people are closer to, or at the center of power. These people have the ability to get things done and to change things to your advantage. This proximity will shorten the time it might take to advance your sales campaign, a significant gain for your selling effort.

When your contact is too low, it is too far from the center of power. Your sales campaign will start in slow motion. You may someday get where you are trying to go, but for the moment, the lower level contact must maneuver and jockey for position with the people who are closer to the center of power. This takes time.

Larger Opportunities

When you approach the executive level in your initial approach, the size of the opportunities will expand. The executives have the ability to see a much larger picture of their company and their budget. They will be concerned with larger and broader issues involving their whole company. The result is that the size of the opportunities you will find at the senior levels will be larger than at the lower levels.

Confirmed Opportunities

When your initial contact is at the higher levels, you will more quickly realize if there is an opportunity to pursue. You will also realize more quickly when there is not an opportunity worth pursuing.

Imagine your prospect already has a similar offering in place. If someone at a lower level in the organization told you that they are satisfied and happy with their current provider, you may give up without knowing the whole story. You may give up not realizing that this information was invalid. For example, the information may be based on nothing more than a personal relationship between the lower-level contact and the vendor. You may give up not knowing that the executives are not happy at all with their current relationship. By calling higher, the quality of the information is better and you are clearer, sooner about your potential success with the prospect.

Stable Relationships

By initially calling at the higher levels, your sales effort will gain stability. The higher-level managers and executives are more in control of their own space and can therefore create a longer-term continuity for your sales campaign. At lower levels, there is usually more movement. Any change in the org chart during your sales campaign would destroy the momentum you developed. The lower-level person is not in control of their space. They serve someone else's agenda. They have little or no control on the agenda of their company or department.

Lower Level Approach

When you approach a company at the lower levels, you are more likely to have a conversation with someone. These people are not as insulated as their seniors are and will have a tendency to answer their own phone.

Another advantage of a lower level approach is that they might be willing to share information with you. They might tell you what the issues are in their company. Unfortunately, the quality of their information is less reliable than if it came from a senior manager. There are very few advantages to a lower level approach.

High-level Approach

High-level cold calling is just that, high-level. This means that your initial contact should be at the upper management or executive level. The offerings you sell are larger and have a greater economic potential. Your approach must be customer oriented and at a business level. Usually, the lower-level person is not interested in this type of approach and will not be receptive. Calling low is only an option when all attempts at higher levels have been exhausted.

You are a high-level professional with an economically impressive offering. You are asking the prospect to shift budget from a current supplier or create new budget. In either case, it will take a powerful ally to do this for you. You are likely to find that kind of power at the highest levels. Lower-level people are functionary in their responsibilities. They are engaged in the execution, not the creation, of their company's agenda. The likelihood that this person has enough power to shift or create budget is unlikely.

Audience Selection

Who is the best audience for your offering? Who is most capable of understanding and appreciating your customer value oriented approach? Since you would like to minimize the amount of time it takes to find new prospects and to begin to do business with them, how can you get the most out of your prospecting activities?

The first guideline for choosing the right audience is that your offering must be a relevant business issue to the prospect. This is a vertical question of how high up the org chart you should be calling. If you are selling a large, supply-chain management software platform that would dramatically change the way a company does business, your target audience is not a software geek in the IT department. This person is not concerned with how their company does business, only with the software functionality of their platforms. The appropriate audience would be much higher, at the very top of the whole organization. Contacting the CEO in this type of situation with a well-crafted CVO approach would be appropriate.

If your offering is something of less importance to the executive level of the target company, then a lower-level audience is appropriate. The central question to answer as you try to determine your target audience from a vertical perspective is this: At what level does your offering cease to be a business issue? Moving up the org chart, at what level is your offering no longer of any business consequence?

The answer is that your target audience is higher than the end user, the implementer or even their managers. The usual answer, particularly with large, complex offerings that demand a more professional approach, is that the target audience is high up the org chart.

The next guideline as you select your target audience is to call the person who is responsible for the function that would benefit the most from your offering. This is a horizontal issue; calling the person who would have the greatest appreciation for your offering. For example, it is very common for IT services vendors to sell to the IT department, calling directly to the CIO. However, the CIO would actually have the most to lose if the services were bought and implemented. They could potentially lose budget, headcount and control of some, or in some cases, all of their formal responsibilities. The CIO would not be the appropriate target.

The final guideline for selecting your target audience is when in doubt, call too high, not too low. If you are unsure who the ideal audience is for your initial call, choose the higher, not lower position.

Call Preparation

You have now decided that it is a good idea to make the call to higher levels in the customer organization. You have identified the person you are going to contact. Before you make the call, do your homework. Prepare yourself to carry on a business level, customer-oriented conversation.

What is the industry of the prospect? What kinds of issues are currently driving that industry? What are investment analysts saying about the industry? If the company is a publicly traded company, what are the investment analysts saying about the company itself?

Then, consider the prospect's role inside the company. If it is a CIO, there is a language they speak and a list of role-specific concerns that you should know about before you make the call. Whether your target is the CEO, COO, CIO, CTO, CMO or CxO, each position has a different set of concerns. You may not get it completely right, but if you are even in the ballpark, the relevance of your call just went up by 100%.

The industry – What is the current economic environment of your prospect's industry? What do analysts think about the future of the industry? Are there any major shifts in terms of technology affecting their industry? Are there business combinations going on? What are the leaders in the industry doing that might be helpful to understand?

The company – What has the recent performance of the prospect company been? Are they suffering compared to their industry? Are they industry leaders? Have they been competently handling recent shifts in their business, or are they distinctly in catch-up mode? If they are a public company, what have their recent financial reports revealed that might indicate a need or a problem that you or your offering may be able to address? What can you learn about their corporate agenda? What have the recent comments by the Chairman or the president indicated about their corporate priorities? Can you identify and understand their major corporate initiatives?

The person – What do you know about the person you are attempting to contact? How long have they worked for the company? Where did she/he work before? Who recruited him/her into the company? Who would be your next choice to contact? Do you understand this person's relationship to the corporate agenda? Is she/he central to the high corporate priorities?

Your value – What is your Declaration of Value for this company? What is the potential financial impact of your offering? Has the customer bought similar offerings before? Do you have experience or knowledge that would be of interest?

Follow-up activities - What are you going to ask the person to do for you? Can you describe the value development process that you would like them to follow? What are you going to ask the person to do if they do not appreciate or understand your value proposition? What are you going to ask the person to do if he/she refers you to someone else in the organization?

By using this type of checklist for every high-level prospecting call that you make, you are increasing your ability to connect in a meaningful way with the person that can make or break your sales campaign.

Mental Framing

You are a professional. You are not an "I don't know; I don't care" cold caller. You are deeply concerned first for the customer's success and then, if it is appropriate and warranted, for your own success. You are seeking a conversation; you have not called to sell them something they do not need. You are not yet in sales mode, you are in discovery mode.

Your approach is professional. Your approach is ethical. Your approach is as considerate to them as you would like them to be to you. You are approaching another executive contemplating the potential of creating new sources of value for them and for you. Your approach is as if you were the CEO of your company and you would like an informal discussion about the potential of doing business. You are not calling to pitch a product, but if they were to ask, you are prepared to describe your offering in high-level, business-oriented language, not tech-talk.

What Do You Want?

Imagine that you have made the call to the executive and you got past the gatekeepers. You have had a conversation and you have reached agreement that some potential for creating mutual value actually exists; now what? What do you want that executive to agree to? What do you want from him? It is critical to know what you want, because he may not have any idea of how to proceed.

You must have a clear idea of what you would like that person to do for you. How would you like to proceed? His question is, "What are you asking for? What do you want from me?" What you are asking for, of course, is not an order. What do you want that person to do for you?

The usual answer to this question would be a meeting; you would like that person to take time out of his busy schedule so that you can sit down with him and discuss and explore business opportunities. You would like to understand his business, his company and his opportunities. You would like to move forward to discover some mutual business opportunity. You would like a face-to-face, in-depth conversation that would not be appropriate over the telephone.

By the end of this proposed meeting, you are going to have to give them guidance on how best to proceed. This will most likely involve other people and resources from their organization and from your organization. You would be looking for this person to introduce you to other people who would be tasked to enter into a discovery process with you. The goal of the discovery process will be to fully define and quantify the value proposition that could be created for their company.

Is this a lot for you to ask a prospect to do? Of course it is. Nevertheless, you are a professional, representing a potential value proposition that might deliver a dramatic and unforeseen financial gain. These types of returns and the investment they require are not sold over the phone or during a single visit to a prospect. They require work, validation, and many other types of consultative behaviors on your part. You will never waltz into the prospect's office and waltz out of there with an order.

Resist the temptation to launch into your product pitch. If you do, you will ruin the business status that you have worked hard to establish. Even if they invite you to talk about your offering, do not use technical language. Keep the dialog on the business level. Talk about the parts of their business that would be affected. Use business language to describe your offering.

Be prepared to describe to them in realistic terms what the buying process involves. You are launching a discovery process with them and their organization, a process that is complex. Describe what the deliverables from that process will be. You may think this might scare them off, but you are actually being very professional in doing so.

Scripting the Call

It is ill advised to write a script and read it to a prospect on the phone. At these levels, and with the preparation you have already done, you should have a very good idea of what you would like to cover in this, your first conversation. People can tell when you use a script. It is a clear indication that you lack understanding.

The exercise of writing down the key points you wish to address before making the call is not a bad idea if you have had little experience talking with higher-level managers and executives. It will help you clarify what you need to say, especially in the opening few seconds of the call. It will require you to think through your conversation to its logical conclusion. It will make you more comfortable as you carry on the conversation. It will better enable you to guide the conversation in the direction that you would like it to go.

The critical thing about scripting, if you feel one is required, is to throw it away before you make the call. Do not have it in front of you. You may want your key points in front of you on a cheat-sheet for quick reference as you make the call, but as you gain experience even that should become unnecessary.

The Opening

Assume that the person you have targeted has just picked up the phone. You know that you have less than fifteen seconds of opportunity when the person is not sure whether to listen to you. What are you going to say in those fifteen seconds while the window is still open? How will you justify that person's investment of more time in this conversation in a concise, professional manner?

As a professional salesperson, you have to establish your credibility and your value proposition quickly. The opening of your conversation needs to be concise, professional and to the point. Your opening must establish a strong enough potential value to make the rest of the conversation a good investment for the prospect.

Three things must be present in those first fifteen seconds. You first introduce yourself, then you must offer the listener a business value, and you must respectfully request to continue the conversation that you are starting. Your opening needs to cover those three components quickly and professionally.

The Introduction

The introduction is simple and straightforward: "Hello my name is...." It is just like those stick-on tags that people wear at receptions. Introduce yourself and the name of your company, nothing more. Anything more begins to sound like an advertisement or a case of nerves: "Hello, my name is Billy Bob Monroe. I work for Gumbo Gadgets, the company that brought you the Wacky Wall Walker" is not a good example of an introduction. "My name is Billy Bob Monroe with Gumbo Gadgets" will suffice, the simpler, the better.

It is best not to use any title at this point. Force the listener to position you at a level in your organization based on the words you choose and the message you send. They will assume that you are selling something, but they might think you are the CEO. Even if you were the President of

Gumbo Gadgets, they would know that you are a salesperson. Whatever spin-worthy title your company has invented to call you will not convince the listener otherwise. Do not use a title at all.

The Potential Value

The value part of your opening is what makes the investment of more time in this conversation a worthwhile affair. The words that you choose in this part must be professional, realistic, credible, compelling and demonstrate to the listener that a few minutes with you in a conversation about the creation of business value is a worthwhile investment. He will be skeptical and somewhat uncomfortable, of course, because he has every right to be. You have invaded his current line of thinking and you are asking him to make a short, unplanned detour in his busy day, so skepticism is natural and to be expected.

This potential value is the same as the Declaration of Value that you use in a CVO approach, with one minor change. The Declaration of Value has three components, credibility, business contribution and financial impact. The difference between the usual Declaration of Value and the one used in an initial call is the use of the qualifier "potential". "The potential exists..." is the type of language you should use.

For example, "Based on our work with customer interface platforms in the airline industry, the potential exists for you to improve customer satisfaction resulting in higher margins." The first part establishes credibility through your experience. You are isolating a business contribution, customer satisfaction, which will be compelling to the customer. Finally, you are identifying the financial impact, higher margins, that could result from working with you.

Another way to express your potential value in your opening is the Trend Identification statement. In this expression of value, you are establishing your business credibility by identifying a business trend that would be relevant to the prospect.

In the Trend Identification statement, your expression of value would contain three things, a trend, a financial impact and a business contribution. For example, "In our work with manufacturing companies, we have seen a shift in the way companies work with their suppliers. I believe the potential exists for you to improve your operating margins by implementing an integrated supplier network platform."

You are identifying a current industry driver that relates to your offering, a financial impact and an area of business improvement that you could potentially offer them. Instead of citing your experience in an effort to establish credibility, as in the first example, you establish credibility because you are aware of a business trend.

Notice that neither of these expressions of value includes any numbers. Using numbers at this point is not wise. Some people might think it is a good idea to suggest gains of X% or X amount of money in the hope that it will generate interest. As high-level salespeople using the CVO approach with a high-level audience, you do not know at this point whether you represent any value, much less 20%. You do not know if your offering will be able to generate the kind of returns it has in similar situations because you do not know how the customer is currently solving the related business problem. Even if you are 100% confident in a specific gain, using numbers to generate interest usually reduces your credibility. You are trying to open a CVO dialog with the customer, using a credible, consultative approach. Numbers will not impress.

Permission to Continue

The last part of your opening statement is a request to continue this conversation. Some salespeople might want to ask for an appointment at this point, but, realistically, you have given the listener no compelling reason to accept an appointment. Your immediate challenge is to get this person to stay on the phone with you for a few more minutes to develop some areas of common interest. That is the most you should hope for at this point.

The request is for a couple of minutes, right now, to develop more clearly the concept of value that you and your offering may potentially represent to them. Do not ask, "Is now a convenient time?" or, "When would be a convenient time?" because "convenient" is a killer word and "convenience" is not the issue. It is never convenient. The issue is value, not convenience. Is it worth the time or not? The convenient question, so overused by salespeople, has made the response almost reflexive: "Not now, NOT EVER." Do not give them the opening.

Your choice of words, as you request permission to continue, is crucial. You finally got the target on the phone and you have already disturbed his previous momentum. "I would appreciate just a few moments of your time, to give you a clearer sense of the value that we might be able to create for you."

As far as openers for initial high-level cold calls are concerned, this is a professional, compelling and concise format. You need to be proficient and relaxed, not inept and nervous. You want to establish, not destroy credibility. You want to appeal to a business issue with a potential financial gain. This is only the opener, what comes next is where your research and your talents count.

Prepare for the Response

You might hear hundreds of potential responses after your opener and a "Yes" is only one of them. In fact, "Yes" is the least likely response you should expect. You should expect the listener to be incredulous; you should expect the listener to be put off; you should expect a negative response.

The potential responses (forgetting the infinite well of human creativity) fall into two groups: positive and negative. The negatives sound like "No time, gotta go," "No," "You people...," "How'd you get my number?" The positives might be less creative. However, in either case, you need to be prepared to continue the conversation.

Negative Responses

The most likely category of responses is the negative response. Your response is an empathy/response format; first, you empathize, then you respond. The empathy part begins with the words "I, too...", and then repeat back, essentially, whatever their objection was to you. "I, too, would feel totally put off by this kind of solicitation call. But..."

The second part of the empathy/response format would be to reorganize your message again. After all, you are a high-level, professional salesperson. You have gone to a great deal of trouble and time to get this very carefully selected senior manager or executive on the phone. The investment of an additional sixty seconds is minimal compared to the potential gain that could come.

As a professional salesperson, any kind of rejection from this audience should be expected. Were you they, you would be in a hurry to hang up, too. However, two things might surprise you. First, senior executives, as busy as they are, realize the importance of politeness. They can be very cordial and understanding. In addition, many senior executives have a background in sales, so they are likely impressed, silently, by your approach.

The senior manager or the senior executive did not rise to their position by making enemies. They are skilled politicians, able to turn away unwanted intrusions with a polite, nearly warm rebuff. The rebuffed might even feel acceptance, as they move on their solitary path - "You have failed, yes, but move on 'grasshopper' and prosper."

Many executives have a background in sales. As a minimum, more and more companies are coming to the realization that the selling organization is a central part of their success. The executives, even in their negative responses, are likely intrigued with the fact that you, somehow, got through to them on the phone. They will secretly wish that more of the salespeople in their company would do the same.

Of course, there will be those few higher-level people who pride themselves in crushing the "little ones" who dare to approach. Fortunately, these are more the exception than the rule. If they are in this category, then their executive ego is not manageable, and your investment would yield naught. Move on to other approaches in the same company or to other companies entirely.

The "No time" response is common. You are a high-level, professional who has gone to a great deal of time and trouble to understand your potential value to this particular customer. As with the "No" response, this is best handled with an empathy/response format: "I, too...." "Time is a precious commodity that requires careful management. If I didn't think that my potential value proposition was worth your time, I wouldn't have called you."

Your research is impeccable and it will only take you a few minutes to deliver your message. "This is going to take less than two minutes and is potentially very valuable. If you're not intrigued by my value proposition and if you do not wish to continue this conversation, we'll both be on our way, but since we're already here, why not take another minute or two?" Of course, now you are obligated to offer a concise and commercially compelling value proposition.

If it were genuinely inconvenient, instead of asking when it would be more convenient, ask if he can see any value to a later conversation. This question acknowledges the presence of enough interest to continue the discussion. You could also ask if there is someone else you could speak with. Either way, you confirmed a level of interest that warrants development. More has started with less.

Another common negative response is the "You people" response. The complaint is that the executive receives hundreds of these phone calls every day/week.

This is a common complaint and is completely justified with all the solicitation calls that come into homes and offices. Again, the empathy/response format is an elegant way of working through this problem. The empathy part might be "I, too, get many of these calls, and I apologize that this is the approach that I felt was necessary to get my message directly to you, but…"

An interesting negative response is the, "How'd you get my number?" response. The question has a tendency to unbalance you, requiring you to detour your intended conversation and loop back to answer a different line of questioning. Answer the question directly, honestly and without any form of evasion. Do not evade the question; answer it and then use the empathy/response format.

Do not forget that you are a professional, high-level salesperson who has done research to prepare for this call. You are not randomly cold calling numbers out of the phone book. You are not randomly selecting strangers in the hope that they could possibly benefit from your offering. You are confident in the potential value for this customer and are determined to get your message across. How you came by their name and number is inconsequential to the value you represent.

Whatever the negative response you get from this type of call, first empathize and then see if there is any way of moving the conversation forward for at least a few more minutes. Do not stop the conversation by accepting the first negative response. You are not going to be able to build any kind of business by prematurely extricating yourself. Quite simply, your livelihood depends on it.

Positive Responses

As important as handling negative responses is the way you handle positive responses. You must keep the conversation at a business and professional level at this time. Even though the response was positive, you only have a limited permission to continue.

Your response to the tacit permission is to thank the executive and continue. "Thanks very much" and then move forward to your value message.

However, just because the prospect has indicated that there might be some level of interest, you may not, under any circumstances, launch into any form of product or technology pitch. Launching into the product/technology pitch will only confirm their suspicions about you and give them the right to excuse themselves from the conversation. You are calling to a senior manager or executive. They have neither the time nor the interest to engage in the minutiae of your offering. That is not how you will successfully connect with this audience and move forward in the discovery process.

The Declaration of Value

The Declaration of Value is the reason they would engage with you in a discovery process. This declaration is a pre-defined statement of the potential and unconfirmed business value that your offering may represent. A carefully crafted statement will quickly reveal the potential business improvement to expect from doing business with you. The Declaration of Value is the result of your research and experience in your company's dealings with similar companies.

The words that you select will provide the prospect with the reason to proceed to the next step, a meeting. The words may be, "Based on the experience we have in the implementation of supply chain management consulting and software, the potential exists for you to gain production efficiencies through closer communication with your suppliers resulting in lower production costs, improved profitability and reduced time-to-market." The declaration must be compelling from a business perspective, and must be tailored for each prospect.

If the prospect indicates that there is no reason to continue, deal with it by disclosing your research and your interest. "I have carefully researched your company and feel strongly that there is a meaningful business gain for your organization in your supply chain management. I understand that I could be completely wrong about my conclusions. What have I missed in my analysis?" This, or something like it, could lead to recovery and a new line of revealing dialog with the prospect.

Do not resort to the "salesy", idiotic questioning concept that some people do, "If I could show you gains of X% in your supply chain management system, wouldn't that be interesting to you?" That type of question is so didactic and condescending that the ire it creates is the ire you deserve. Even though many salespeople use this type of blunt-force question, its use at the senior management or the executive level is not advisable. It is insulting.

If the prospect's response to your Declaration of Value is positive, be prepared to explain more fully your value in business terms. You are still unclear of the potential business gains in this situation and you still have no clear idea of how much business gain would result. You are beginning the discovery process with the prospect to define and quantify a business result.

The ideal outcome from the Declaration of Value for you would be for the prospect to ask the question, "How are you going to do that?" A well-crafted Declaration of Value hopes to develop interest in starting an exploration to define and quantify the financial gain by adopting your offering. Be prepared to give a general overview of your offering in business terms and to describe the discovery process. Resist the temptation to launch into a product or technology pitch. This is not the time.

Probative Questions

Based on the research you did to prepare for the call, be prepared to ask several questions to begin the discovery process. These questions need to be business-related and will serve to demonstrate to the prospect that you are genuine in your belief that business value could be created. Your questions could follow several lines: financial impact, business process impact or the impact on their customers or market position. Prepare your questions in advance, based on the research you have done. How do they measure financial impact? What are their core financial measurements? What are their high priority initiatives? What are their major concerns?

Be prepared to ask good questions. It might even be a good idea to try the questions on a colleague or a manager before using them in conversation. Some questions look good on paper, but when posed only serve to hurt your credibility. How you frame these questions is very important as well. Address your questions to the business, framed in a positive, future-oriented context.

Your Ending

You have reached the point where you should logically move on to the last step of the initial call, asking for the appointment. The conversation has gone well and there seems to be real potential for business gain for the prospect and his company.

However, before asking for the appointment, be prepared to give an overview of how the buying process would proceed. For example, "In similar situations, we have worked with customers to fully define and quantify a value proposition for the platform. This would involve working together to identify and size the potential areas of improvement and would provide you with a clear financial model to either justify the platform, or take a pass on the platform. We can kick this discovery process off with a meeting with you and any others from your organization that you feel should be a part of the process." You have now given the prospect some idea of how you would like to proceed.

They may have a different way they would like to move the dialog forward. Ask for their input on how they would like to proceed. It is a simple and courteous question. As opposed to feeling that you are forcing a meeting, you have given the prospect control of the relationship. "How would you like to proceed?"

Ask for the Appointment

In asking for an appointment, be straightforward and flexible. A senior manager or executive's time is precious and not to be trifled with. Ask when they would like to have the meeting. Do not resort to the silliness some salespeople resort to in asking for appointments. Do not use the, "Is Tuesday afternoon or Wednesday morning best for you?" approach. Be straightforward and professional, "When could we meet?"

If you are traveling to their area for other reasons, say so. "I will be in the area next Thursday. Have you got an hour open to meet?" They might appreciate the fact that you are a businessperson and would like to control your cost-of-sales. However, if it requires a special trip only to see them, then do it.

If taking a meeting with this customer requires you to get on an airplane and fly halfway around the world to meet with them, then do it. If you identified the prospect as being worthwhile for prospecting, then you should already have justified any travel or related expenses associated with converting them from a prospect to a customer.

Finally, how much time out of the executive's schedule should you ask for? There is some debate about asking for a pre-determined amount of time for the appointment. It is courteous of you to say that a set amount of time should be set aside from their schedule. However, some salespeople will ask for too little, "I'll need fifteen minutes of your time to explain…." This is not a good thing, even though many salespeople feel that by asking for only a few minutes, they increase their chances of actually getting the meeting.

In high-level selling, asking for too little time will minimize the relevance of your offering in the mind of the prospect. If it is only worth a fifteen-minute meeting, then the potential financial impact must be minimal.

It is better to ask for more time, rather than less in large, complex sales campaigns. After all, it is impossible to have a relevant business discussion in fifteen minutes when the financial impact could be in the millions. Ask for an hour, maybe two, of the prospect's schedule. Ultimately, the prospect will determine how much time to invest anyway, so asking for what you need is best.

Barriers to Entry

The common barriers to getting to the executive audience are Executive Assistants, Administrative Assistants, Secretaries and Voicemail. Executives have multiple layers of protection around them. The assistants' job is to see that the executive remains on-course, capturing as many profitable hours as possible in a single day. They deal with the noise and chaos surrounding the executive and enable the creation of maximum value.

It is common for these assistants to handle a higher level of responsibility than their title might suggest. In some cases, they are responsible for decisions that directly involve the corporate agenda. These people are talented and capable. They have to be to satisfy the high expectations most executives place on them. They are trusted as confidants with insight and information that is not widely shared.

There are many ideas on how best to get past the gatekeeper to the executive. The best and most professional approach is to treat the assistant the same as you would the executive. As far as you are concerned, they are the executive. Treating them with the same format and the same value messages as the executive is the best idea.

Their job is not to keep you out. Their job is to keep non-essential issues out and allow value and potential value in. Your job is to represent value to them and thereby the executive.

Voicemail is an electronic assistant that allows the executive to screen out the nonessentials and allow value in. Most executives do not even screen their voicemail, their assistant does. Unless you know the private direct line number to the executive's office, then you are bound for voicemail. Just as with the admin and the executive, treat voicemail in the same format with the same value messages.

When All Else Fails

Making contact at the executive level of a company is a hard thing to do. You should never limit your approach to only one avenue at the executive level. It is a good idea to identify several executives and senior level managers that could serve as your entry point. Identify the ideal person for your prospecting efforts, but do not stop there. The likelihood of getting in will increase if you can identify several people as potential entry points.

Even though going in too low is not the best option, it may be necessary at some point. You should try the higher approaches first and give them many opportunities to succeed. However, when all else fails, consider a lower level entry point, being careful not to get boxed in. You may be able to find someone who could help you understand his or her organization. They may even perceive some form of personal gain if you are successful in getting to the executive audience.

Sources of Information

There are many sources for this type of information including services like Dunn and Bradstreet, Standard and Poor's, Moody's Investor's Service, Edgar's Online, and Hoover's Online. Some of these services will even provide the names of the senior executives and contact numbers. There are other companies that will provide you (for a fee, of course) with not only the names of the senior executives and key managers, but also an in-depth background of the company including the analyst reports and opinions, industry analysis and financial reports. Many on-line information sources can help you in your investigation, as well. Sites like Yahoo! and MSN have an investor section where you can research financial information. These sites are not as extensive as the others, but they are free.

Creative Penetration

Be creative in how you might penetrate an account. Are there local health clubs or restaurants that these people frequent? What civic organizations do they participate in? What is the company's favorite participant sport? What are their preferred charities? Find unique ways of getting close to the audience in your target companies.

In the final analysis, you must be in outreach mode on a regular and consistent basis. You must prospect continuously, no matter how successful you are. There is a real distinction between the high-level, value oriented approach and the, "I don't know; I don't care" cold caller. If Bill Clinton, George Bush and Al Gore find making these calls necessary, then you should too.

Competency Development

The execution of this sales methodology requires a high level of competence in the following areas.

High-Level Sales Competencies

Business Acumen is your ability to analyze business problems and create advanced, customized solutions that address specific customer problems. It is your knowledge of accounting terminology and business concepts. It is your awareness of business, industry and market related issues and their impact on your customers.

Political Acumen is your ability to understand quickly and accurately the invisible political structure. It is your ability to recognize the most powerful people and act accordingly. It is also your ability to build and execute a political plan in a responsible and culturally acceptable way.

Relationship Acumen is your ability to develop and maintain professional relationships at the upper management and executive levels. Your ability to understand people, their personal and professional agendas and your ability to engage those agendas is central to this competence.

Strategic Acumen is your ability to understand complex sales situations and act in the most effective way possible. Central to this competence is your ability to analyze the situation and find the best approach to solving problems. It is your ability to develop and share effective strategies. It is your ability to execute the defensive countermeasures required in a high-level sales campaign.

Sales Skills

Closing Techniques in high-level selling is recognizing the appropriate moment to seek closure to a sales campaign. The appropriate moment is when the customer is informed, prepared and empowered to make a buying decision. Unless these specific conditions have been met, asking for the order is pointless. Trial closing, a related concept to closing techniques, is the ability to compel a customer to acknowledge what obstacles remain. Trial closing, to a high-level salesperson, is obstacle analysis, the recognition of remaining impediments to a potential purchase.

Overcoming Objections is the ability to turn around a customer's problem in the contemplation of a purchase. Done well, they can bring about a completely new level of dialog, one of dealing with real problems, not just the problem of a purchase. Overcoming objections, done improperly, can offend many customers.

Negotiation is the ability to advance a dialog with a customer in a professional manner when opposing agendas impede progress. Negotiation addresses the known obstacles to doing business and seeks creative ways of removing them.

Prospecting is not only cold calling but also the initial call to a lead or an introduction. The call's intention is to create interest in doing business. High-level prospecting is a professional value oriented approach to the executive level.

Professional Skills

Writing has become a critical skill for salespeople with the wide acceptance of email. The written word, unlike the spoken word, is a permanent communication and it is critical to success and should not be taken lightly.

Critical Thinking is the ability to clearly articulate a problem and creatively solve it. Critical thinking is problem solving, situation analysis and creative thinking and is important to high-level selling.

Public Speaking is more essential now than ever. Public speaking offers the unique opportunity to persuade en masse, shortening the customer's decision time dramatically.

Basic Concepts of Law are necessary for the high-level salesperson. Understanding the basics gives you the ability to negotiate more clearly and create unique solutions to the problem of doing business.

Business Language is the understanding of accounting terminology, the language and thinking involved in running a business. Understanding the terminology businesses use to measure their financial results will help the high-level salesperson develop a more intimate understanding of their customers.

Corporate Finance is the area of business that involves capital formation and capital management. It is the working of the stock and bond market and the comparison of one investment to another.

Recommended Reading

On Strategy:

Sunzi Speaks: The Art of War by Sun Tzu, Illustrations by Ts'ai Chih-chung, Translation by Brian Bruya, Anchor Books Doubleday

Griffith, Samuel B., *The Art of War by Sun Tzu*, Oxford University Press

Mastering the Art of War, Translated and Edited by Thomas Cleary, Shambhala Publications

Competitive Strategy by Michael Porter, The Free Press

Creating Strategic Leverage by Milind M. Lele, John Wiley & Sons, Inc.

Thinking Strategically by Avinash K. Dixit and Barry J. Nalebuff, W. W. Norton & Company

Say It and Live It by Patricia Jones and Larry Kahaner Currency Doubleday

The Mission Statement Book by Jeffrey Abrahams, Ten Speed Press

On Politics:
The 48 Laws of Power by Robert Greene and Joost Elffers Viking

On Business:
The Discipline of Market Leaders by Michael Treacy and Fred Wiersema, Addison-Wesley Publishing Company

Inside the Tornado by Geoffrey A. Moore, Harper Business

Value Migration by Adrian J. Slywotzky, Harvard Business School Press

Customer Connections by Robert E. Wayland and Paul M. Cole, Harvard Business School Press

The Death of Competition by James F. Moore, Harper Collins

Reframing Organizations by Lee G. Bolman and Terrence E. Deal, Jossey-Bass Publishers

Real Time by Regis McKenna, Harvard Business School Press

Only the Paranoid Survive by Andrew S. Grove, Currency Doubleday

Competing in the Third Wave by Jeremy Hope and Tony Hope, Harvard Business School Press

Leading the Revolution by Gary Hamel, Harvard Business School Press

The Age of Spiritual Machines by Ray Kurzweil, Penguin Books

Business @ the Speed of Thought by Bill Gates, Warner Books

On Selling:
Key Account Management and Planning by N. Capon, Free Press

Rethinking the Sales Force by Neil Rackham and John R. DeVincentis, McGraw-Hill

Let's Get Real or Let's Not Play by Mahan Khalsa, White Water Press

Solution Selling by Michael T. Bosworth, McGraw-Hill Professional Publications

Consultative Selling by Mack Hanan, Amacom

SPIN Selling by Neil Rackham, McGraw-Hill

What's Your Point? by Bob Boylan, Adams Media Corporation